THE EN

TED BUNDY

The Questions and Controversies Surrounding America's Most Infamous Serial Killer

KEVIN SULLIVAN

WildBluePress.com

THE ENIGMA OF TED BUNDY published by:
WILDBLUE PRESS
P.O. Box 102440
Denver, Colorado 80250

ISBN 978-1-952225-38-3 Trade Paperback
ISBN 978-1-952225-37-6 eBook

Interior Formatting/Book Cover Design by Elijah Toten
www.totencreative.com

THE ENIGMA OF TED BUNDY

TABLE OF CONTENTS

PREFACE

I've been writing about Ted Bundy for many years now. When my first book, *The Bundy Murders: A Comprehensive History*, was published in August 2009, I believed it would be the only book about Bundy I would ever write. After all, it's a biography of the killer and a full treatment of the murders, and I couldn't imagine going down that Bundy road again. But six years later, in 2015, I decided to write what I would call a companion volume to *The Bundy Murders* and this became *The Trail of Ted Bundy: Digging Up the Untold Stories*, published in 2016. This was followed by *The Bundy Secrets: Hidden Files on America's Worst Serial Killer*, published in 2017, and in 2019 I rounded the series out with *Ted Bundy's Murderous Mysteries: The Many Victims of America's Most Infamous Serial Killer*.

At this time (and with good reason), I considered myself finished with Ted Bundy's life of murder. However, within two days of the publication of "*Mysteries*", a Facebook friend of mine contacted me and asked if I'd ever considered writing an encyclopedia Ted Bundy. Taken aback, I told him no, adding this new book was just released and the last thing on my mind was yet another Bundy book, and I told him no; at least I said, that's my answer for now. However, over the next several days as I considered the project, I started to feel pretty good about it. Plus, I was aware that there had never been an encyclopedia written exclusively about the Bundy case, and such a book could be a good addition to what I'd already written; and in fact, there was nothing on the market quite like it. And so, in April 2020, *The Encyclopedia of the Ted Bundy Murders* was published.

And now, in what I anticipate will be my final book on the killer, I am tackling a number of questions, speculations, and controversies that have surrounded the Ted Bundy case for many years, and we'll be looking for answers along the way. And because many readers have enjoyed the republication of parts of the official record (and they keep asking for more!) with commentary from me as with previous companion volumes, I'm adding more here; including the surveillance of Bundy by the Utah authorities—something you'll discover that disturbed the killer greatly. And as always, nothing appearing here has appeared in any of my previous works on Ted Bundy, and you'll find these reports fascinating.

It wouldn't be a companion volume without my usual inclusion of the voices of those who were there and crossed paths with Ted Bundy. And along with these, I'll also be including the stories of some who believe they had a run-in with the killer, but their stories cannot always be placed in the category as absolute or verified contacts. Even so, what they have to say is intriguing and of sufficient interest making them worthy of an inclusion here. It is also important to note that the unconfirmed stories within these pages are well within the parameters that it could have been Bundy, as they happened in locations where Bundy lived and operated during his time of murder.

Additionally, I'll also be adding something to this final Bundy book that I've not used in any of my books on Bundy, except in very small quotations only. And that "something" happens to be the taped recordings of the detectives and others I interviewed while writing my book, *The Bundy Murders*, and these tapes have been transcribed in their entirety for the very first time. Indeed, it's been so many years since I've listened to them, I've now learned they contain far more useable material than I realized at the time. As such, they warrant an inclusion here.

Lastly, as with my previous Bundy books, whenever I'm adding commentary to the record, I'll preface it in italics with *Author's note.* When I'm adding explanations to the taped interviews, it will also be in italics, but without Author's note.

CHAPTER ONE

THE OFFICIAL RECORD

Author's note: Because this is the official record, I have left it as it is, without corrections in grammar or those things an editor would do when going over a manuscript. It is important to publish the record as it appears. However, I will note where mistakes are located, as well as occasionally correct a misspelling, as I did with the misspelling of Liz Kloepfer's name. Outside of these noted corrections, the record remains the same as you can see them in the archives today.

Ballantyne Supplementary Report

Attempt to Locate Monday Jan. 26, 1976

On Sunday, January 25, 1976, this officer received a call from Chief Dean O. Anderson stating that Mr. Richard Maughan had called him and advised that Margaret Maughan, his daughter, had some information about the Bundy case.

At 2:30 P.M. on 1/25/76 this officer and Chief Anderson met with Richard and Margaret Maughan in Chief Anderson's office. The following is the substance of Margaret's information.

Margaret stated that she had talked with Ted Bundy and they conversed about the tear in the back seat of Ted's Volkswagen. Ted Stated they can't get me on that because a lot of Volkswagen's have torn back seats. Margaret stated to this officer that she noticed the tear in the back seat just before Ted sold the car and the stuffing was coming out of it.

Ted also advised that he didn't believe there was a difference between right and wrong, and that he liked virgins and he could get sex with them anytime he wanted to.

Margaret advised that the front seat in Ted's Volkswagen was loose and when you rode in it you had to hang on because the seat would rock.

I asked Margaret when she had last seen Ted and she stated just before Christmas. She advised at that time he was supporting a full beard. I asked her if Ted wore glasses often and she stated no but when he does, he wears different types. When asked if Ted had to wear glasses, she stated she didn't know.

Margaret advised that she has talked with a newspaper reporter from Seattle by the name of Henderson (first name unknown) but he writes for the night paper. Mr. Henderson advised that he and Ted had taken a trip down the river in Seattle in a boat. Tied behind the boat was a innertube which a girl was riding on. The boat hit some rough water and according to Henderson, Bundy got a wild look in his eyes and untied the innertube. Henderson further stated that Bundy drove like a wild man back to Seattle, and never said a word for the entire hour and one half.

Further Henderson told Margaret that someone had written down the Washington plate number that is on Ted's truck in an abduction in Oregon.

I asked Margaret if she knew whether Ted had ever been to Colorado and she stated that he had been over to one of the ski resorts.

Ted further told Margaret that he had asked a Carl Weary (spelling unknown) to watch his apartment for him when he left town because he was fearful that the police might try to break in. Ted obtained a heavy lock for the door, put screws in the windows and pulled the ladder up from the window. Margaret will obtain the date this happened.

Ted further advised that he had taken a trip over Lambs Canyon and had come out in Provo in the fall in 1974 prior to the snowfall. I asked Margaret if she knew of it was before or after the disappearance of Debra Kent, but she didn't know.

(*Author's note: what follows is a Bountiful Police report, somewhat redacted, pertaining to a student taking a phone call at Viewmont High School in the days following the abduction of Debra Kent (by Ted Bundy) which occurred on the evening of November 8, 1974. It is an odd call, and in this writer's opinion, it's just the thing Ted Bundy would do. After this incident, the rest of the report continues*)

BOUNTIFUL POLICE DEPARTMENT

Supplementary Report

Wednesday, Nov. 13, 1974.

I interviewed Pam at Viewmont High School and she stated that she works in the office and that at approximately 11:45 A.M. she stated that she received a telephone call from an individual that sounded like an older person, who wanted to know whether or not Debra KENT was at school or if she was on the absentee list. She was asked three of four times by this individual if Debra was at school.

Supplementary Report

Friday, September 5, 1975

Case No. 9340-74

COMPLAINANT: DEAN KENT

Reporting officer, Sgt. Collard, LT. Ballantyne wen to Salt Lake in an effort to locate the car belonging to Theodore Bundy in an effort to have the car observed by Carol DaRonch (*Author's note: Carol DaRonch, whom Bundy abducted from the Fashion Place Mall, and who shortly afterward escaped from her attacker.*)

The car was located at suspects residence. At this time Sgt. Collard went to pick up Carol. Prior to his arrival the vehicle left his residence, went to the university, back to his residence and then down to the telephone office on 200 South and 300 East.

Just shortly prior to Sgt. Collard's return to the area the vehicle left westbound on 200 South. Reporting officer followed and the vehicle turned north on Main Street. Reporting officer was caught in a red light and hemmed in by traffic.

Prior to reporting officer's arrival on Main Street, the vehicle disappeared and this officer was unable to locate the vehicle. This officer checked all known possible locations again and was unable to locate the vehicle.

Reporting officer will attempt to relocate this vehicle again and attempt to have the witness look at the vehicle.

Supplementary Report

Wednesday, September 17, 1975

Case # 9340-74

COMPLAINANT: DEAN KENT

VICTIM: DEBRA KENT

This is an interview of Elizabeth Kloepfer (redacted). She works at the University of Washington Medical Institute. Elizabeth goes by the name of Liz.

Elizabeth was asked when she first became concerned about Ted and as to why she became concerned about him and thought that he might possibly been involved with some of the girls that had been slain in the Seattle area. She stated that she first became concerned because he resembled the composite which had been produced in the Seattle area and in following the newspaper reports she discovered the days the girls turned up missing he was not with her on any of these days.

She stated in October a girl friend of hers whose name is unknown at this time had visited Utah. Upon returning from Utah told her about a similar incident in the Salt Lake area which involved a missing girl very closely resembling that of the ones in the Seattle area. At this time Liz contacted the Seattle Police and advised them of Ted Bundy and asked them to contact the Salt Lake Police and talk with them in regards to him.

She stated that later another girl turned up missing in the Salt Lake area, this one as she recalled approximately Christmas time. At that time, she contacted her dad who was in Ogden, requested he call Salt Lake County Sheriff's Office and inform them of her suspicions. He had told her at this time that he did not wish to do this as he had no evidence and did not wish to become involved with the situation. She stated that when he informed her, he would not do this she herself called Captain Hayward and spoke with him at that time.

Liz was then asked if she knew where Ted received his money for his schooling and other bills. She stated that she did not know for sure. As far as she knew just from jobs he had.

This officer inquired as to whether or not his parents supplied some of the money. She stated she did not think so as they were not wealthy people and his father works as a cook at the Madison (*Author's note: Madigan*) Army Hospital and his mother works as a secretary at the hospital (*Author's note: University*) at Puget Sound and they live on a moderate income.

Liz was asked if she thought Ted was being truthful with her. She stated no. She was asked as to why she thought this. She stated that she knew he had lied to her in the past. She stated he has stolen items in the past such as a television and a stereo, a bicycle and possibly other items and at that time he had lied to her.

She was asked if she knew when he had purchased the vehicle, the Volkswagen, he is presently driving. She stated he had owned the car since approximately 1972. She stated the color was a light beige at the time.

She stated he purchased a white Ford pickup truck which he has presently in the Salt Lake area about one year ago before he left for Salt Lake City. (*Author's note: I was recently told that the white truck went with Bundy to his 364 Douglas Avenue residence, and that the vehicle remained in the rear of the home, and perhaps in the garage, for quite some time after Bundy was incarcerated.)* She was asked if she had ever gone skiing with Ted. She said she had gone skiing one time at Snow Basin; however, she could not remember the date. She also drove up to Snow Bird with him last year, however, it was too crowded and they did not go skiing. She was asked when the last time was that she saw him and she stated in August of 1975. She was asked if at that time they had gone to the Park City area. She stated they had not. She did state, however, they had spent some time at Flaming Gorge at her dad's trailer.

She was asked if he liked the outdoors and she stated he did like the outdoors very much. Liz was asked if Ted had asked her anything about any of the girls that had been slain. She stated that he knew he was a suspect in the slaying of some of the girls in the Washington area and that he has known this for approximately 10 days to two weeks as someone has been in contact with him from the Washington area who has been contacted by the Seattle area police. She was then asked if he had said anything to her in regards to being a possible suspect in any of the girls in the Utah area. She stated he had not.

She was then asked if she knew whether Ted travelled much. She stated he was not much of a traveler. As far as she knew he did not travel very much at all. She was then asked if she was very close to him. She stated she was very close indicating that they had in the past had sexual relations. She was asked if over the past year he had changed and she stated no.

She was then asked if she felt he sometimes had two different personalities or acted like two different people.

Her response was I think he is now. She was asked why. She stated that she has of late seen a side of him which is very cold and calculated. Liz was asked about how her father got along with him or what her father thought of him. Liz stated her father gets along well with him; however, he thinks he is just an opportunist that is taking her for a ride. When asked if she felt this way she stated well, he always ate at her house and at that time, they talked of plans for the future, which would include plans for marriage.

Liz was asked how long she had worn her hair in the style she is presently wearing it which is long, dark brown hair parted in the middle approximately shoulder blade length. She stated she has worn this for approximately the last six years as long as she has known Ted.

She was asked if he liked the way she wore her hair. She stated that she had at different times stated she was going to cut it which he became somewhat upset stating he liked it that way and not to cut it. She also stated that he had dated one other girl she knew and she also had long dark hair.

Liz was then asked if there were any unusual sex hang ups that she was aware of. Her first response was he has a normal sex life and then went on to elaborate that at the end of 1973 he asked her one night if he could tie her up for the sex act, that he used her nylon socks to tie her with and laying her on the bed he tied her legs spread apart and then tied her arms and hands. She stated that he also developed a liking for anal intercourse during this same period of time.

She stated that she only allowed him to tie her up a couple of times but the last time he tied her up while they were in the act of their sexual relations that he placed his hands around her throat choking and hurting her, however, at that time she did not say anything to him in regards to this, however, she refused to be tied up any more after that. She stated he had obtained these ideas from reading a book which he had purchased by the name of "Joy of Sex".

She stated that one thing that bothered her was that during the summer of 1974 that his sex drive dropped to near zero. She stated that one possible explanation was that he was working quite hard and was tired a lot of the time. She stated she had confronted him as to whether he was possibly having an affair with other girls to which he stated no.

Liz also stated that one day as she entered his apartment, she found a brown paper sack in the middle of the floor just inside his apartment door and she noticed one of the items in the sack was a woman's bra, however, she did not go through the sack any further. When asked why, she stated she did not know, maybe she was possibly embarrassed or scared to do this. She stated this was in the fall of 1973. She stated she did not ever say anything to him about it and he did not ever say anything to her.

Liz was asked if Ted had any knives. She stated he always had knives. When asked what kind of knives she stated he had an oriental type knife which was in a wood sheath which he kept in the glove compartment of her car for several months. At one time she had asked him what it was and he stated it was just a knife that a friend had given him.

She also stated he had a meat cleaver in his apartment that he kept with his other cooking utensils. Liz was then asked if there were any other unusual items, she knew of in his apartment that she did not know he had. She stated she had found some plaster of Paris which would be used for a cast possibly. When she stated when she asked him why and where it came from he stated it was something he swiped from a medical supply house he worked for near the University of Washington. She also stated he had a pair of crutches. When she confronted him with them, he stated they were the landlord's and he had left them in his apartment.

Liz stated she had received a phone call from Ted last date in the evening. She was then asked if he had mentioned anything about Salt Lake or the police in Salt Lake. She stated he had. She had confronted him in regards to his arrest and he became quite upset because of her knowing it. He stated the police had contacted Seattle and Seattle was doing some checking on him and the police in Salt Lake were harassing him. He stated the officer that arrested him was out to get him and was just plain harassing him.

She stated he also said that the police had over-stepped their bounds and he was not worried about the charge he was picked up on because it was an illegal search (*Author's note: notice he's not saying he's not worried because he's innocent, only that they made a mistake - which they didn't - and it's a technical issue.*)

Liz then inquired as to whether all the items were together in a bag indicating the handcuffs, the ski mask, etc. She was told in the affirmative. She stated that she had confronted him in regards to the items she knew were in the bag and that he had told her he used the ski mask to keep his ears warm while he was shoveling snow as it was cold. She did not know at that time about the handcuffs or some of the other items in the bag.

Liz was then asked if she knew whether Ted wore patent leather shoes very often. She stated she never knew him to wear patent leather shoes at all. She was then asked if she had ever known Ted to wear a mustache. She stated she has known him to wear a full beard, however, never a mustache alone. She did state however he always had a fake mustache. When asked what style she described a brush type. She stated he had owned this ever since she has known him for approximately the last six years, and that he usually carries it with him. When asked why he had it she stated he sometimes wears it to act cool.

Liz was then asked if she knew of the rip in the backseat of Ted's car and she stated it had been there approximately one year. She was asked if she knew it was fixed and stated she did not. She stated he was planning on selling his vehicle to help pay for his tuition and lawyer. She stated when he talked with her last date he also asked her to send him $700.00 to help pay for his lawyer. She then stated she inquired of him why he was carrying a crowbar in his car. He stated he always carries a crowbar and in fact he stated he used it the day before he was stopped and did not state what for. She stated she asked him why he had run from the officer. She indicated he told her that he had been drinking beer and didn't want to stop.

Liz was then asked where Ted had resided prior to his coming to the Seattle area. She stated he had been in Philadelphia for a while approximately seven or eight years ago going to a university there.

Liz was then shown a picture of a girlfriend in the Salt Lake area of Ted's and asked if she knew her. She stated no. She then asked is she a close friend of his. She was informed that it is thought that she is.

She stated then that Ted in his conversation with her had indicated that the police in Salt Lake knew he was coming to Seattle to sell his car and he was wondering how they knew. Liz was then asked if she knew Ted had joined the Mormon Church and she stated she did. He had told her the Missionaries had been on his back ever since he had got there and he had decided it was the right time to join.

Liz was then asked if she knew how he knew the police knew he was planning on coming to Seattle to sell his car.

She stated she did not and the only possibility she could think of was possibly her old bishop as he had asked her how to contact him as he wanted him there for the baptism.

Liz stated he has called her several times this past week always telling her how much he really misses her, that he needs her and wants her to marry him. She stated he has not done this in the past and this seems unusual to her.

Liz was then asked if she would classify him as a schizophrenic and she stated I do now. She was then asked if she would classify him as being somewhat schizophrenic during the sex act and she said no. She was asked if she could think of anything else unusual. She stated in trying to think back and remember as near as she could recall she had received a phone call that she thought was a Friday night as near as she could remember which was the same night that one of the girls in the Salt Lake area disappeared, possibly, that of Debra Kent. She stated it was unusual for him to call from a pay phone.

She was asked if he had ever been violent and had ever hit her. She stated he had not. The only time he had hit her they had been out drinking one night, got into an argument and she stated go ahead and hit me and he did.

Liz was then asked if she knew if he owned a gun. She stated as far as she knew he did not. She was then asked if she knew of any unusual mental hang-ups that Ted might have and she stated the only thing she could think of was that he was an illegitimate child and that his mother had never told him. He had learned of it and he was quite embittered about this, however, she stated as far as she knew his mother did not know that he knew about this.

Liz was asked if she knew of any other things that Ted might of stolen. She stated one time a police officer came to her house stating that someone had pawned a stolen camera using her address. She stated it was described as a guy who at that time was with a blond girl and she is now wondering if Ted might have possibly been the one to pawned it.

Liz was then asked if she had any doubts in her mind in regards to Ted's activities. She stated she has a lot of doubts and she is definitely not sure and she at this time could in no way marry Ted and at this time any thoughts of marriage are out.

(*Author's note: what follows is a re-interview of Liz conducted the next day, September 18, 1975.*)

This is a re-interview of Elizabeth Kloepfer – known as Liz.

This took place at the University of Washington Hospital at 11:00 Hours 9/18/75

Interviewers were: Reporting officer and Detective Deputy Jerry Thompson.

Liz was asked as to her knowledge of the attitude toward police officers in general and she said Ted has a very good attitude and is usually praising police departments. Liz was then asked Ted's habits towards mixing with groups and she stated he mixes quite well, however, he does not have a lot of close male friends.

She was asked what type of sports he participated in and she stated tennis and handball. She stated she did not know of any other particular ones than this.

Liz was asked what contact she has had since September 1974 with Ted. She stated she has talked with him several times by telephone and in December 1974 at Christmas time she came to Salt Lake. In January of 1975 he visited in Seattle between quarters and in August of 1975 she again visited him in Salt Lake City. She stated while she was visiting him in December in Salt Lake, she learned Ted was smoking a lot of pot with his roommate or acquaintance that lived across the hall from him by the name of Scott. She stated this was always a problem between them after she learned it and they argued considerably about him using marijuana and the effects it could possibly have on him.

Liz then referred back to the picture which was shown in the last interview and asked if that girl's name was Gloria Ann or Glory Ann. She was told no it was not. She stated that he had developed a friendship with a girl by the name of Gloria A. who is a law student at the University of Utah as they worked together on several projects for class.

Liz was then asked if Ted had ever mentioned to her anything in regards to the missing girls, especially in the Washington area or Salt Lake area. She stated he has talked to her about the girls in the Washington area, however, he has not talked to her very much. He stated since the time he was arrested in Salt Lake he has talked to his ex-landlord in the Seattle area who had been contacted by the King County Sheriff's office in regards to a background check on Ted and that his landlord had told him he is being investigated in the possible disappearance of the girls. He stated he had discovered it is not a good thing to be named Ted in the Seattle area.

She stated he had contacted a friend of his by the name of Ann Rule who lives in Seattle and who writes crime stories for magazines and that Ann contacted King County to see what was going on and they told her it was strictly a routine investigation. She stated Ann re-contacted Ted and informed him of such.

She was asked if Ted had mentioned anything to her about the type of evidence the police had in regard to the disappearances and slayings of the girls and she stated he has not.

Liz was then asked if she had ever known Ted's car to be any other color than the beige color which it presently is. She stated she has not that it was beige when he got it. Liz was then asked if Ted ever mentioned any girls or types of girls which he does not like or any types particularly that he likes and she stated he has not.

Liz was then asked what her girlfriend's name was to which she had referred to previously that she had discussed this situation with. She gave the name as Mary Lynn Chino who lives at (redacted)...When Liz was asked if her girlfriend Mary Lynn had any doubts towards Ted, she stated Mary Lynn definitely has some doubts.

Liz was then asked again in reference to a raft which she stated Ted had. She stated he has a four-man yellow rubber raft which she had given to him as a graduation present when he graduated from the University of Washington.

Liz was then asked if Ted had ever mentioned being to Bountiful or knowing anyone in the Bountiful area and she stated he has not.

Liz was then questioned again in regards to the mustache. She stated it was a brown mustache. It was straight and quite sparse brush type and just came to the corner of the lips and did not drop at all.

In reference back to the night of 9/16/75 when Liz had talked with Ted, she stated he had lied to her about being arrested. But when she told him that she knew that he had been arrested he stated he had been arrested for speeding. She then informed him that she knew why he had been arrested and he became quite upset at her knowing. He then stated that after they had stopped him they had gone through his car looking for anything and everything to bust him on and he was surprised that they had not taken the fire extinguisher out of his car and charged him with arson also.

At the time Liz talked to him she did not know anything about the handcuffs and therefore did not ask him anything about it. Also, she stated that her car had been stolen for a few days in the summer of 1973 and was gone for two or three days and when the car was returned the oriental type knife in the wood sheath was missing at the time. She stated that Ted did drive her car occasionally.

Liz was then asked if Ted had ever been to California. She stated Ted had been to the San Francisco area in the spring of 1973 for a few days on business. She did not know anything more about his visit there.

Liz then stated one thing that struck her funny that she had talked with Ted in June (*Author's note; the transcriber typed J ne, so it must be assumed he meant to type June.*) and he was talking about hearing one report on the radio in regards to several rapes which had occurred in 1st Avenue in Salt Lake which is near the area he lives. The description of the guy involved was a guy with a beard and he stated to her I guess that lets me out. He stated that he thought a possible suspect was an individual that lives in a house for mentally retarded people around the corner from him which would be on F Street and that right after this description came out this individual shaved his beard and head. Liz, he stated, isn't that kind of funny (?). Liz stated that she told him not any funnier than a guy that is growing a beard. She stated Ted grew a beard in June 1975.

Liz then referred to a question that had been asked in an earlier interview in regards to two separate Ted's or schizophrenic personality. She stated that in thinking back Ted is very jealous of her. He follows her when she goes to various places or meetings to see who she is with or what she is doing. She stated he takes naps and sleeps a lot during the day and is out a lot late at night. She stated he used to sneak up on her when she was walking alone at night when she had no idea he was around and suddenly jump out of the bushes and grab her scaring the hell out of her.

She stated that this really made her angry. Liz referred back to the girls which were missing from the Seattle area stating that the only one she could really pin-point was one on July 14, 1974 which turned up missing shortly after she started becoming suspicious of Ted.

She stated on Saturday night they had been out and had argued. On Sunday morning she was starting to get ready for church and that Ted came over which surprised her due to the fact she thought he was mad at her. She stated he asked her where she was going to which she told him to church and then another place she was going and she thought he might meet her there, however, he did not. She stated approximately 6:00 PM that day he came over and asked her to go out to dinner with him. She stated at that time she had asked him where he had been as he looked very beat. He told her just laying around.

Liz was then asked as to her opinion of Ted's sexual activities, as to whether he as a very virile man was able to have repeated intercourse with only a few minutes in between. She stated when they first met he was able to perform very well, however, after six years of knowing him she stated she feels he is just a normal man. Liz was then shown a picture of the items which were confiscated from Ted's vehicle at the time of his arrest. She was asked if she had ever seen the crowbar before and she stated she had not and had no idea of his having it. She stated the only thing she has ever seen before is the gloves and the bag and the rest is foreign to her.

Liz stated that the items did look very suspicious and could cause some concern. Liz then stated there was another item which she could think of that might be somewhat suspicious. She stated when Ted used to drive her car around, she noticed he had taken her handle for the jack and had taped the one end of it. This being the end that curves slightly with adhesive tape and she had found this inside of her car a few times and not just in the truck area. She stated she had asked him as to why he had taped the handle and this occurred during the time there were student riots at the university and he stated with the riots you never know when you might need it.

She stated another incident that one night he was at her house, that he left, then came back shortly after. He returned to the porch and took something from an urn on the porch. She opened the door and observed the action but was unsure what it was and when she asked him what it was, he looked sick and tried to hide it from her. She stated she grabbed it from him discovering it was a pair of surgical gloves. She asked him what they were for and he just turned and left. This she said was one night late at night.

Liz then referred back to December and she had read or heard from somewhere that one of the individuals in the Salt Lake area was supposedly wearing a trench coat and when she flew into Salt Lake and Ted met her at the airport he was wearing his trench coat telling her how much he really liked it and enjoyed it. She stated she was quite struck when she saw him in the trench coat due to the fact that he had heard or read this previous to her coming down.

Liz then stated that after Ted learned that the police had talked with his landlord about him he called her and told her that if the police should try and contact her and talk to her that she was not to talk to them without first obtaining a lawyer. She stated she asked him what do I need a lawyer for, I haven't done anything wrong. She stated he told her that he just didn't want her to talk to the police without having an attorney present. (*Author's note: Bundy was thinking like a suspect here; suspects need attorneys when questioned by the police, not a couple of landlords merely answering questions about a former tenant. As if Ernst and Freda Rogers would put up a stumbling block between them and the police, and hire an attorney out of their own pocket. The truth of the matter is this: Ted Bundy spent his adult life asking things of people, be they favors or money, and whenever he felt like he could get away with it, would tell people what to do – for him! – and this is a perfect example.*)

Liz was then asked if Ted was a frequent visitor of the State Park where the girls disappeared in the Seattle area. She stated he was not. The only time she had ever known him to be there was approximately one week prior to the disappearance of the one girl (*Author's note: an obvious mistake here, the officer knowing -and stating above- that two women disappeared from the park*) from the state park area. She stated at that time he had gone there alone.

Liz then stated after having talked about the items which have been discussed in the interviews both yesterday and today her doubts are greatly increasing towards Ted and she wishes she could know for sure and at this time she has considerable doubts. She is of the opinion that there is a great possibility that Ted might be possibly involved in this.

(Author's note: what follows is a detailed report of a meeting Lt. Ballantyne and Det. Jerry Thompson had with Charles and Rose Marie Shearer who were friends of Ted Bundy in Utah. Small portions of this report (and other incidences not found in this report) have found their way into other reports that have been used in one of my previous works on Ted Bundy, but because this is a substantial report and has information not used in my previous books, it's worthy of an inclusion here. Lastly, there will be a number of errors of grammar and typos, but because they do not cloud or misinterpret the actual meaning of the writer, I have left them as they appear in the record, except for the name "Belknap" which was incorrectly spelled, "Belnap". No other changes were made.)

Reporting officer, Lt. Ballantyne and Deputy Jerry Thompson of Salt Lake County Sheriff's Office went to (redacted) (*Author's note: this would be 565 First Avenue, Bundy's rooming house in the university district.*) where contact was made with Rose Marie Shearer in (redacted).

After Mrs. Shearer agreeing to speak with these officers was asked how long she had lived there and she advised approximately 3 months. She was then asked if she knew Mr. Bundy. She stated who?

It was then asked if she knew Ted Bundy and she stated she knew Ted as he acted as manager of the apartments and he was the one who had showed them their apartment.

She was then asked if she knew if he had moved. She had stated he had moved approximately one week ago. She was asked if she observed him moving and she stated no.

It was inquired as to who the landlord was and she advised a Mr. Belknap at Badger Realty. (*Redacted*).

It was then inquired if she knew Ted had sold his car and she stated she did not, however, she stated he might have as she had not seen it for a while. It was then asked if she was very good friends with Ted. She stated they had talked with him a little bit but did not really associate too much with him. It was inquired if Rose Marie lived there alone and she stated no she was married and lived with her husband.

This concluded the interview with Rose Marie Shearer.

As reporting officer, Lt. Ballantyne, Detective Thompson were leaving the Shearer apartment, Mr. Charles Shearer came out stating that he did not want these officers bothering his wife or his family as to what Mr. Bundy's problems were and he did not wish to become involved.

Mr. Shearer was asked if he would be willing to talk with these officers and he stated he would. Mr. Shearer then indicated that Mr. Bundy had informed him and one of the other neighbors that they were not to drink beer out on the front porch or in any way antagonize or give the police a reason to come to the residence as they had been following him around and was constantly roaming around the apartment.

Mr. Shearer stated that he had been aware that there had been what appeared to be plain clothes officers sitting out front and also around the apartment building.

Mr. Shearer stated that he then went to Mr. Bundy's apartment and inquired as to why the police were watching him as to whether or not he had done anything or if it might be someone else they might be watching.

He stated the Feds were after him due to a tear in the back seat of his car and the tools that the police found in his car which they claimed were burglar tools and that they were trying to pin some killings of some girls on him due to these things.

Mr. Shearer then stated that he had sold his car approximately two weeks ago for approximately $700 to $750 to a young lady who has a small child, however, he did not know her name. (*Author's note: this was a lie to keep the truth of where the VW was and who actually purchased it; this way the authorities would have a difficult time locating the car. The buyer was actually a 17-year-old by the name of Bryan Severson. There is much more to this story, and you can read the complete details of Severson's involvement in the case in my book, The Bundy Secrets: Hidden Files on America's Worst Serial Killer, published by WildBlue Press.*) It was inquired as to whether Mr. Shearer was good friends with Ted. He stated he had talked with him several times. He stated in his opinion Ted was two different people. When asked what he meant by this he stated he just acts queer sometimes.

One night he left approximately 1:00 a.m. and when he returned approximately 4:00 a.m. he just burst right in his apartment even though his wife was in bed. When asked why he had done this he stated he thought they might be up.

He also stated that Ted would sit and drink beer with them and then suddenly he would for no reason at all would state that he was indulging too much and would have to quit that kind of stuff. He just seemed to have two personalities.

Mr. Shearer also stated that Ted had from time to time indicated that he enjoyed going to one of the local bars called The Sun Bar which is supposed to be known as one of the local queer joints. He stated he would not even go there if he knew there were straight people there. This is all the information that Mr. Shearer could give.

Contact was then made with Margarete Maughan in (redacted). Miss Maughan stated she had been a friend of Ted's approximately a year and they had moved in (*Author's note: this would be 565 First Avenue, Salt Lake City, Utah.*) together about the same time. Miss Maughan seemed quite reluctant at first to speak with these officers as she stated she was a good friend of Ted's and did not wish to get him in trouble.

She stated that she was quite surprised that this investigation was still going on, that she had been aware of plain clothes policeman around the apartment and following Ted. She first became aware of this when Ted first told her about it. She stated she had been in Canada at the time Ted had been arrested.

She had stated he had told her he was out for a ride and wanted to go to Heber, however, he did not have the money so he rode around the valley. He stated he had been out in the Kearns area and noticed a vehicle coming up on him rapidly from behind and he started out and then the red lights came on indicating a police car and he pulled over and stopped.

He stated that they went through his ashtray trying to find marijuana seeds and could not find that. The Highway Patrolman then told him that he was the same vehicle that had evaded him earlier and he was then arrested for evading.

Miss Maughan stated that as far as the ski cap, the ropes and the crowbar that Mr. Bundy was quite an outdoorsman and that these items along with a blanket were used and kept in his car for emergency purposes in case he was caught out in the cold overnight, and these could be used for survival.

Miss Maughan was asked if she knew where Ted was living. She stated she did but did not know if she wished to reveal this to these officers at this time. After several minutes Miss Maughan stated that she wanted to cooperate, however, she did not want to feel she had given the address out and that these officers were going to continue to harass Ted. Miss Maughan then gave the officers the address which was (redacted- *Author's note: this would be Bundy's 364 Douglas Avenue address near the University of Utah.*) This address was verified that this is where Ted is living.

Miss Maughan also indicated that she planned on contacting Ted and advising him that we were still inquiring and interested in him.

Deputy Thompson contacted Mr. Belknap of Badger Realty who advised Deputy Thompson that Mr. Bundy had given him the keys on Tuesday night of the last week and that he had checked the apartment finding it very clean and he did not have to do further cleaning. He had shown the apartment on Wednesday, rented it and the new tenants had already moved in.

As of the writing of this report the vehicle has not been located.

A subpoena was then served on the University of Utah and a copy of Mr. Bundy's records was obtained.

Reporting officer contacted Deputy Ben Forbes, Salt Lake County Sheriff's Office and inquired of him as to any information he received from Washington in regards to Theodore Robert Bundy. He stated the only thing he had received was that on 10/18/74 Mr. Bundy had called his girlfriend in regards to making arrangements to go deer hunting with her father. Her father flew into Salt Lake City on 10/19/75 (*Author's note: this is a typo. It should read 10/19/74. In October 1975, Bundy would be charged with the abduction of Carol DaRonch and placed in the Salt Lake County Jail.*) and was picked up by Mr. Bundy at the airport and at that time traveled to the Logan area where he spent the next three days hunting.

Deputy Forbes also stated that Deputy Jerry Thompson is presently checking all phone calls on Mr. Bundy's phone bill with a subpoena from the court and also all credit cards, to determine where Mr. Bundy has been traveling and what dates as he is using a Chevron Credit Card.

At this time there is no further information, however, reporting officer will be checking into all leads on this individual.

Party Interviewed: Janette Benson

Interviewed on 10/10/75 at 0930 Hours

Janette was asked when she first met Ted Bundy. She stated it was in January at the beginning of the second semester. She was asked if she had known or seen him during the first semester. She stated he may have dropped into class a couple of times but she did not actually meet him to where she knew who he was until the second semester.

Reporting officer asked her if she recalled seeing any scratches on Ted's face and she stated that she could not recall seeing any scratches at all. Reporting officer asked if she had done any work projects related to school with Ted and she stated she had been scheduled to do one, however this did not materialize and therefore she did not do any.

She stated that her association with Ted was strictly social contacts being at various social gatherings which he also attended.

Janette was asked whether or not she felt Ted mingled well with crowds. She stated he mingled very well and was always associating with the people at the gatherings.

Reporting officer asked Janette if she had observed anything unusual about Ted's actions. She stated she had not. She stated the Ted she knew was a very well mannered, polite fun person to be around. Janette stated there was nothing further she could offer.

This terminated the interview.

(*Author's note: When I wrote The Bundy Murders: A Comprehensive History, I added several pages to the book detailing how the Washington state authorities surveilled Ted Bundy when he returned home (having made bail in Salt Lake City, Utah) in November 1975. And because that proved to be of great interest, as the surveillance was taken directly from the officer's reports, I would publish all of the remaining Washington surveillance reports in a later companion volume published by WildBlue Press. As such, I believe it is fitting (because this is my last book on the Ted Bundy case) to present the similar reports, recorded by Utah law enforcement as they surveilled him in Salt Lake City in the late summer and fall of 1975, prior to his last trip home to Washington State in the aforementioned November of 1975.*)

September 10, 1975

Case: Surveillance in regards to the Debra Kent and Melissa Smith case.

Case # 74-59463 & Case # 9340 -74. Surveillance team is Sgt. H.O. Collard and detective Ira Beal of Bountiful City.

Surveillance was set up on the above date at 0805 a.m. At 0805 the suspect's Volkswagen License # LJE379 was parked in front of the apartment complex directly East of his residence. His white Ford Pickup is parked to the rear of his apartment complex.

Suspect at 0935. The suspect left his house and proceeded to 5th Avenue and F Street, entered Smith Food King and remained there for approximately 5 minutes, returned to his vehicle and went south on 5th Avenue to 1st Avenue. At 0940 the vehicle was eastbound on 1st Avenue, turned south on F Street. Vehicle eluded pursuing officers at 4th East and South Temple.

At 1125 the subject returned home. Surveilling officer was facing mostly on 1st Avenue on the Northeast corner. As soon as the vehicle which approached home from the East traveling West pulled into the driveway. Surveilling officer then pulled into the parking lot across the street. He observed Mr. Bundy enter the home at which time entered the home with a package of groceries and then approximately 10 seconds later, came back out of the home. Subject then left his home and traveled East on 1st Avenue to "I" Street and then South on "I" Street to the next street running East which he apparently took East. Approximately 1135 the subject was observed walking West on 1st Avenue directly in front of this officer's vehicle. This time the officer's vehicle was parked in a parking lot on the Southeast corner of 1st Avenue and "I" Street. The Vehicle was parked in the furthest North portion of the parking lot facing North where the subject's home could be observed. Subject walked West bound on "I" Street, approximately 5 feet in front of the officer's vehicle to the corner of "I" Street and then he walked South, came back to the parking lot and stood at the rear corner of the officer's surveillance car where he appeared to be taking note of the license plate number. (*Author's note: this frustration that Bundy experienced while being "spied upon" by the police, always birthed an intense aggravation within him, leading to displays of noticeable nervousness by the officers as well as juvenile reactions from the killer; reactions, such as the Washington State cops would experience a few months later when he returned home for the last time: writing down their license plate number or taking pictures of the officers or their vehicles. Now, one would be inclined to think that since Bundy could take all the pressures surrounding murder (planning the hunt, deciding where to murder, whom to murder, and the discarding of the remains), a little pressure being applied by law enforcement during surveillance, wouldn't bother him at all. The truth is, the authorities were very pleased to see the killer under this pressure, as they understood he'd be less likely to kill again during this time where he was being closely watched*). At this time the subject then walked West towards his home. This was the last time the officer observed him.

Assisting units which were enroute from Bountiful were then contacted at 1150 and advised of the situation. At 1305 hours, reporting officer then made contact with Mr. Morton of the Morton Insurance Company on South Temple which is about 650 East South Temple and made arrangements for the use of his office space. A picture was then taken from this location of the home. At 1315 hours, reporting officer then went next door to the second floor of the Fireman's Fund Insurance Company where another picture of the home was taken and an attempted picture was made of Mr. Bundy who was then seated in the upper left hand windows, which is his neighbor's apartment, sitting looking out the window with his neighbor who is a white male, American, approximately 5'11, 170 lbs., with a light brown or blond hair. On this occasion the neighbor was wearing a rust-colored shirt and Mr. Bundy was wearing a blue shirt with blue pants, light in color. Arrangement was also made at this time to utilize the upper floor during the evening surveillance of (*Author's note: the writer means from)* the Fireman Fund Insurance Company. At 2:25 p.m., confirmation was made with officer Beal on the fact of Mr. Bundy's car still being at the rear of his apartment house.

At 2:35 p.m., contact was made with Sgt. Holt of the Salt Lake County Sheriff's Office and he was given the telephone numbers of 531-1234, & 355-4651 which belonged to the Morton Insurance Company in the event that he or his oncoming afternoon shift needed to contact this officer. At 5:10 p.m. this reporting officer along with officer Harwood of the Salt Lake County Sheriff's Office observed Mr. Bundy pull his car from the rear parking area of his apartment down to the sidewalk where he was once again in his coveralls, and appeared to be working on the bumper of his vehicle. It should be noted at this point the bumper was observed to (be) back on the vehicle and also on the bumper was located the correct license plate that matched the rear license plate. The License number being LJE379. After turning over the keys to the building to Detective Harwood of the Salt Lake County Sheriff's Office, this reporting officer left the Salt Lake area at approximately 5:15 p.m.

Case is still active.

Reporting officer is Sgt. Collard of the Bountiful Police Department.

Surveillance Team: Sgt. W.O. Collard, Detective Ira Beal, Detective Art Stones.

A joint meeting was held at approximately 8:00 a.m., at the Metropolitan Hall of Justice with Captain Pete Hayward after which surveillance was set up in the area of I Street and First Avenue. This took place at approximately 9:40 a.m.

While setting the surveillance up it was determined that the subject's vehicle, a beige Volkswagen, was not in the area at which time an attempt was made by Sgt. Collard at the University of Utah to locate the car. Attempts were made by Detective Beal and Detective Stones to locate the car in the area of downtown Salt Lake City.

At approximately 2:30 p.m., reporting officer made contact with Detective Thompson who advised Reporting Officer of the subject's telephone number. This number was called and there was no one found to be at home.

A telephone call was placed at approximately 2:45 p.m. As of this time, which is 2:45 p.m., there has been no further contact with the subject or his Volkswagen.

At approximately 2:50 p.m., the girlfriend's Datsun, which is dark blue in color, was observed at the back of the residence. It was not observed coming in or out of the area by the officers on surveillance.

As of 4:10 p.m. officers on surveillance have not made contact with the subject or his vehicle and as of 4:10 p.m., the dark blue Datsun, which was identified as belonging to his girlfriend, who lives directly below him, is still located at the rear of the apartment complex.

THIS CASE IS ACTIVE.

Surveillance team with Sgt W.O. Collard, Detective Art Stones, and Deputy Detective J.R. Hunt.

On September 15, 1975, the above officers set up surveillance in the neighborhood at "H" Street and 1st Avenue at 8:15 a.m. At approximately 8:45 a.m. subject got in his car and drove south on 700 East to 800 south where he traveled west to Green Street where he stopped for approximately five minutes. The home at this location is a multiple dwelling and the addresses which may have been visited by the subject are as follows: 651, 653 or 647 or 649 East 800 South.

The vehicle then left, traveled east on 800 South to the second home east of 200 East on the right-hand side of the road. At this location the vehicle then parked. The individual then walked across the street and talked to a man and a woman. The location address would be 727 East 800 South.

The man was described as male, approximately 6'3", 200 Lbs., with blond hair. The address of this individual would have been a multiple dwelling also being either 713 or 715 East on 800 South.

At approximately 9:10 a.m. the officers lost contact with the subject vehicle in the area 800 South 700 East. The vehicle was then picked up again at 9:30 a.m. at the subject's home by Detective Hunt. When the subject returned home, he entered the home and came out with a passenger and went for a short ride. This would have consisted of having traveled north on "H" Street from 1st Avenue to 3rd Avenue and then east to "K" Street where he then turned left, traveled north and then to approximately to 5th Avenue, made another turn to the left and came back down "J" Street and south on 1st Avenue back west to his home. There were no stops made and no real reason for the chase other than the fact that it is felt by observing officers that he is extremely paranoid and that either suspects or is aware that he is being followed.

At 10:00 a.m. he came out of his home and walked to the store and went inside at this time. He was wearing a red and black plaid shirt, red gym shorts and tennis shoes. This was observed by Officer Hunt. At approximately 10:03 a.m. the subject returned home.

At 10:45 a.m. subject came from the apartment with a brown case which was approximately 1 ½ feet high, 1 foot wide and 2 feet deep. At this time, he visited with another tenant who had just traveled to the drugstore and bought a Coke and was sitting on the front porch of the apartment house. The individual is the one with the curly black hair and a mustache.

The subject was then followed to the University of Utah where he parked west across University Avenue across from the Law School, at approximately 10:10.

At this time the subject got out of his vehicle, walked north on University Avenue to 200 South then west to 1300 East and then back east on 200 South to University Avenue. And the whole time he kept looking around constantly. This officer observed him from about 3 blocks away from the circle in front of the University of Utah Administration Building.

The subject then appeared to observe this officer approximately 3 blocks away and began walking towards this officer's direction at which time this officer pulled out on the one-way street and left the "U". Reporting officer then returned to the area at the east of the law school where he parked his car and entered the building directly south of the law school in order to keep surveillance on subject's vehicle.

While inside this officer was notified by Detective Stones that subject came walking by Reporting Officer's vehicle and examined the interior of that vehicle. This officer then observed the subject traveling west on 400 South towards University Avenue, then north to his car. He then backed his car up approximately four parking spaces to the north, got out and went back into the law school building.

At about 11:45 a.m. subject left the law school, walked north on University to 200 South and then walked west to 1300 South and was last seen at this time at 300 South and 1300 East by Detective Hunt.

Approximately 10 minutes later which would have been 11:55 the subject was observed down in the area of 1100 East and 400 South, walking around and looking up and down the streets. At 12:15 the subject returned to his car and went home. He was at his home for approximately five minutes and then departed.

The subject was lost at approximately 12:25 in the area of the avenues and contact was lost until approximately 1:25 p.m., at which time his car was found parked at University Avenue and 300 South. This officer then took up surveillance of the subject's vehicle on University Avenue. Officer Hunt drove his car to the top of the circle in front of the University Administration Building and sat. At approximately 2:00 p.m. Officer Hunt observed the individual behind his car taking a picture of his vehicle and walking up and attempting to take a picture of himself.

At approximately 2:10 p.m. the officers met and discussed the situation at which time we decided to return to Bountiful. In returning, this officer drove down University to 200 South, subject's vehicle was still there.

Reporting officer then observed the subject standing in the middle of the intersection at 200 South and University Avenue with his camera. As the officer passed through, he attempted to take a photograph of this officer and his vehicle.

The subject during the course of the day appeared to have accomplished nothing more than trying to evade these officers and trying to catch the officers as they were holding surveillance. His actions indicated that his purpose at the University was not one of study or attending any classes.

The subject is extremely concerned about being followed or watched and has a most suspicious nature about himself.

(Author's note: What follows is a Utah court document that is an interesting summation of the Carol DaRonch abduction, as well as other interesting tidbits of the case. For example, in my book, The Bundy Murders, I state that when Officer Bob Hayward arrested Bundy in the early morning hours of August 16, 1975, Bundy had been smoking marijuana, as can clearly be seen in the document (Bundy admitted it), but others have said this isn't so. That said, this should clear things up. Plus (and only in some circles), it has been alleged that Bundy never owned a pair of patent leather shoes. Well, Jerry Thompson said that the first time he was at his apartment he saw a pair (Carol DaRonch said he had a pair on the night she encountered him), but the next time he was there, they were missing. And in the ensuing years, some believe Thompson made a mistake. Well, this document reports that two residents of 565 First Avenue (Bundy's rooming house) have testified that Bundy did in fact own a pair of patent leather shoes. As a coincidental aside, I just noticed that I requested this document on August 16, 2006 – 31 years to the day from when Bundy was arrested in Granger, Utah by Utah Highway Patrol officer Bob Hayward.)

Wed. Aug 16, 2006 at 2:29 PM

108Q3J

Print Request: Selected Document(s): 5

Time of Request: August 16, 2006 02:28 PM EDT

Number of Lines: 158

Job Number: 1842:113718357

Client ID/Project Name:

Research Information:

5 of 6 DOCUMENTS

STATE of Utah, Plaintiff and Respondent, v. Theodore Robert

BUNDY, Defendant and Appellant

Nos. 14741, 15534

Supreme Court of Utah

589 P.2d 760; 1978 Utah LEXIS 1500

December 28, 1978, Filed

SUBSEQUENT HISTORY: [**1]

Petition for Writ of Certiorari to U.S. Supreme Court Denied April 30, 1979.

COUNSEL:

Bruce C. Lubeck, John D. O'Connell for Defendant and Appellant.

Robert B. Hansen, Earl F. Doruis, and R. Paul Van Dam, for Plaintiff and Respondent.

JUDGES:

Ellett, Chief Justice, wrote the opinion. We concur: J. Allan Crockett, Justice, D. Frank Wilkins, Justice, Gordon R. Hall, Justice, F. Henri Henriod, Retired Justice. Maughan, Justice, having disqualified himself, does not participate herein.

OPINION BY:

ELLETT

OPINION:

[*761] The defendant was charged with, and convicted of, the crime of aggravated kidnapping. The trial was to the court sitting without a jury. An appeal was taken to this court however, before the appeal was heard, counsel for the defendant claimed that he had newly discovered evidence which would warrant a new trial. This court, having

confidence in the integrity of counsel, remanded the case on his motion to the district court where a hearing was had on the motion for a new trial and for extraordinary relief. The district court judge took evidence and heard arguments and finding the motion to be without merit denied it. An appeal was taken from that ruling to this court and [**2] the two appeals are now consolidated for our consideration.

The matter of granting or refusing to grant a new trial lies within the sound discretion of the trial judge and we will reverse his decision thereon only where he has abused that discretion. n1 In this case there was no abuse of discretion.

- - - - - - - - - - - - - - Footnotes - - - - - - - - - - - - - - -

n1 Kettner v. Snow, 13 Utah 2d 382, 375 P.2d 28 (1962); Haslam v. Paulsen, 15

Utah 2d 185, 389 P.2d 736 (1964).

- - - - - - - - - - - - End Footnotes- - - - - - - - - - - - - -

As to the facts of the case as revealed at the trial, the judge, as a trier of those facts, could readily have found beyond a reasonable doubt, and did so find, that an 18-year-old girl was in a Shopping Mall where she was approached by a man who told her that someone had been trying to break into her automobile. She thought that he was a police officer. The area was well lighted and she stood face to face with him while they talked. The man asked her to accompany him to the car to see if anything was missing.

Upon reaching the car the girl looked in, determined nothing was missing, and so advised [**3] the man. He then told her that the alleged burglar was being held inside the mall, and once inside, the appellant told the girl that "they" must have taken the suspect down to the substation. He and the girl then walked straight across from where they had just entered the mall and walked around the building by a clothing store. Appellant asked her how old she was, if she was doing anything later that night, and why she would not be able to "go over there" and sign a complaint against the person who had allegedly tried to break into her car. This conversation occurred while the two were walking, with the girl slightly behind the man. The girl noticed the way he walked and that he was wearing green pants. Later at a lineup, she identified the appellant as her assailant immediately upon his entering the room because of, among other things, his manner of walking. She also observed that at the time of the offense he was wearing dark patent leather shoes, and that he was slim, weighing about 160 pounds, had greased back hair, and had a dark mustache which did not extend past the corners of his mouth.

She and the man walked to a nearby laundromat. The man tried to open the front [**4] door, found it to be locked, walked halfway down an alley between the laundromat and an adjoining building, turned around and came back. During this period of time, the girl again observed appellant's facial features as he was standing "right in front" of her in very good lighting conditions. She became suspicious of the situation and asked appellant if she could see his badge or some form of identification. He produced a wallet with a badge inside. She [*762] described the badge as "thinking it was silver, kind of oval shaped."

The man then asked her to accompany him to the police station and fill out a complaint since "they probably had him (the alleged burglar) down there." They walked to his car, described by her as a Volkswagen with a rip on the top of the backseat, rust spots on the front, no license plate, and of light color, either white or beige. The rip was described as going "almost all the way across" the top of the backseat.

They drove a couple of blocks to a school where appellant abruptly stopped, parking the car partially onto the curb. The girl nervously asked him what he was doing and why he was stopping because this was not a police station. The man [**5] grabbed her left arm and forcefully placed a pair of handcuffs on it. She grabbed the door on her side, managed to open it and get one foot out. The man grabbed her by the arm and around the neck. She kept screaming, "asking" him what he was doing. He then pulled out a gun, pointed it at her, and said he was "going to blow her head off." She managed to get out of the car but the man pursued her. They struggled outside the vehicle as she tried to free herself. She grabbed his arm and right hand and then felt an iron he was holding in his hand. She described it as having four or six sides, about one-half inch thick. Her impression was that the object was a crowbar since her father had one which she had felt before. To keep the assailant from striking her with the crowbar, she held it with her left hand.

She continued to scream "as loud as I could." She then testified that she turned away "pulling and scratching." Her fingernails, long at the time of the trial, were even longer the night of the incident and were broken in the scuffle. She recalled scratching the assailant during the fighting because she remembered noticing that all her fingernails were broken.

She finally [**6] succeeded in breaking away from her assailant. She ran into the street, the handcuffs still dangling from her arm. She managed to get a car to stop for her. She jumped into the car, related briefly what had occurred, and requested them to take her to a police station. They drove her directly to the Murray Police Station.

At trial, the State and appellant's counsel stipulated that up to this point, the amount of time during which the girl had been with her assailant was between ten to fifteen minutes.

At the police station the victim was questioned by three police officers, one of whom removed the handcuffs which were both on the same wrist.

There is no contention made that no crime was committed. The defendant simply claims that he did not do it. Two witnesses who lived in the same apartment with the defendant testified that he wore patent leather shoes on occasion.

There was human blood on the sleeve of the victim's coat which was type O.

The defendant's blood type is O; that of the victim is type A.

Approximately nine months after the assault, at 2:30 a.m. on August 16, 1975, appellant was driving his Volkswagen in a residential area in Granger. Sgt. Robert Hayward of [**7] the Utah Highway Patrol, sitting in his patrol car, observed the Volkswagen pass him. Approximately five to eight minutes later, Sgt. Hayward started his car and while rounding a nearby corner, again observed the Volkswagen at the side of the street. As the patrol car approached, the appellant took off at a high rate of speed with his headlights off. Officer Hayward gave chase. Appellant subsequently ran a stop sign in an attempt to evade the officer. Finally, appellant brought his Volkswagen to a stop.

Sgt. Hayward exited his car, approached the Volkswagen, and observed a "jimmy type pinch bar" (crowbar) behind the front seat on the back floor. He asked the appellant what he was doing in the area and then inquired, "Can I look in your car?" Appellant's response was, "go ahead." Sgt. Hayward stated that at no time did the appellant object to the search. The appellant was then placed under arrest for evading a police officer.

[*763] Moments later, Deputy Sheriff Twitchell and Sgt. Fife of the Salt Lake County Sheriff's Office arrived on the scene and were advised of the situation. Deputy Twitchell then asked the appellant "if he would mind if we looked through his vehicle." [**8] Appellant responded that "it was okay with him." Officer Twitchell further testified that to the best of his recollection, he did not remember appellant objecting to the search of his vehicle at any time. Appellant, a law student, denied giving his consent and testified that he passively stood by because he was intimidated.

A search of appellant's vehicle by Deputy Twitchell and Deputy Ondrak, who arrived subsequent to Deputy Twitchell and Sgt. Fife, produced a pair of handcuffs and the crowbar located on the floorboard behind the driver's seat. Deputy Ondrak testified that he remembered appellant's Volkswagen as being tan in color.

The victim had described the Volkswagen driven by her assailant as being a light color (white or beige); at one time she had said the car possibly could have been light blue but later eliminated that possibility. In connection with this, it should be noted that Mary Walsh, the first person to talk with the victim following her assault and kidnapping, testified that any confusion regarding the color of the Volkswagen driven by the assailant could be due to the type of lighting in the parking lot at the Mall which makes a car seem to be a different color [**9] than it really is. Also, a lady who lived downstairs from appellant in the same apartment building at the time of the kidnapping, testified that she had been in the appellant's car two or three times during the months of October and November of 1974, and that the color of appellant's Volkswagen was cream-color. James Dunn, a neighbor of appellant's, testified on his behalf, and although he admittedly may have been "kind of" color blind, he believed the appellant's Volkswagen to be "beige, light-colored."

After Sgt. Hayward was joined by the other deputies and officers at the scene, they asked the appellant what he was doing in that neighborhood. The appellant told the officers that he had attended a movie and then had gone for a drive. Appellant admitted at trial that this was a lie and further testified that he had also lied to one of his attorneys concerning the events of the evening of August 16, 1975.

When questioned at trial about the evening of August 16, 1975, appellant said the reason that he sped away from Sgt. Hayward was because he was "smoking dope" and did not want to be caught doing something illegal.

His final version of the events of that evening was that he [**10] was eating dinner and watching television until 12:00 midnight or 12:30 a.m., at which time he decided to visit a friend. Upon arriving at his friend's house, he noticed the lights were out. He decided not to awaken her and proceeded to drive around for a while, ending up in the Granger area where he decided to smoke some dope. He said he fled from the patrol officer in order to dispose of the marijuana and to open the car window in order to air out the interior of the automobile. The arresting officer testified that he saw nothing thrown from the fleeing car and that there was no smell of marijuana on the defendant or inside the car; and that he was well acquainted with the odor of marijuana. Two other officers at the scene of the arrest testified to the same effect as did the arresting officer.

At a pretrial hearing on a motion to suppress the evidence relating to the crowbar and handcuffs taken from the defendant's car, the trial judge found by a preponderance of the evidence that the defendant had consented to the search of his car and denied the motion to suppress. An acquaintance of the defendant testified that the defendant told her that he let the officers search his [**11] car when he was arrested.

The defendant, some five days after his arrest, gave the police permission to search his apartment. The search revealed several pairs of patent leather shoes. The officers also took several pictures of defendant's Volkswagen. The victim recognized the rips on the back seat as being like those she [*764] had observed while being held captive in defendant's car. She testified at trial to the same effect. She further testified as to dents and rust spots on the Volkswagen as being the same as those observed at the time of the crime.

Other evidence given at trial clearly connected the defendant with the crime charged. It is not necessary to detail the incriminating evidence any further. The evidence already set out was sufficient to justify the judgment of the court.

Counsel for appellant complains because the court permitted the prosecution to discuss the probabilities of defendant's guilt by referring to various aspects of the evidence. The prosecutor's argument was proper for while any one circumstance might not convince the trier of the facts beyond a reasonable doubt, a great number of circumstances, taken together, could do so.

The claims [**12] of error have been carefully examined and we find no merit to any of them. The judgment is therefore affirmed.

It is to be noted that Mr. Bundy had fled from Utah and is now in the State of Florida where he is awaiting trial on charges of murder.

WE CONCUR: J. Allan Crockett, Justice, D. Frank Wilkins, Justice, Gordon R. Hall, Justice, F. Henri Henriod, Retired Justice.

Maughan, Justice, having disqualified himself, does not participate herein.

(*Author's note: The last document I want to present is a detailed report from King County detective, Kathy McChesney. I will not be using all of it, as some of it I've used in previous books and I don't want any redundancy. Some sections of the report dealing with particular individuals, I'll be using in their entirety, but others only various paragraphs of interest. In some cases, I'll be using snippets only. And to show breaks in the report initiated by me, they will be followed by an ellipsis. A note: McChesney misspells Liz Kloepfer's last name, so I have corrected this.*)

Det. K. McChesney
10-9-75 0830 hrs.

0900 hrs. R/O had phone contact with Liz Kloepfer. On July 14, 1974, Ted called her about 5:00 p.m. and came over about 6:00 p.m. They went to the Greenlake Bowl for hamburgers, shifts were changing there about that time. Ted was very hungry. They went to Farrell's and then back to Liz's where he took the ski rack off his car and put it on hers. He didn't feel well and he went home. They did not have sex that night. It was about 9:15 p.m. that he left for home.

The photo of Bundy was taken in 1971 or 1972, that was shown to witnesses in which Ted is wearing a white t-shirt. On occasion Ted would use Liz's credit card to purchase gas…Liz's mother kept a diary and some information was obtained from her by Liz. Liz's parents drove to Seattle on May 23rd, 1974 and stayed until June 3rd. They stayed at Liz's house. On the evening of May 31st, Friday, Ted took Liz and her parents to Pizza and Pipes for dinner. They were there about 1 ½ hours and then Ted took them home and went home himself. Liz talked to him sometime the following afternoon and at 4:30, Liz, her parents and daughter went to church. About 5:20 (20 minutes late) Ted arrived. He stayed for the baptism and then returned to Liz's for dinner. After dinner Liz believes Ted stayed a long time and then they fell asleep on the floor watching television. Ted went home about 11:00 p.m. The following Thursday Ted didn't work and accompanied the family to Dungeness Spit on the Olympic Peninsula.

During the time Liz's parents visited they didn't use Ted's car to go anywhere. Also, he didn't say why he was late for the ceremony (*Author's note: baptism*)…

…Received call from Det. Jerry Thompson, Salt Lake City. He verified that Bundy's passenger seat was removed and on the back seat and the burglary tools was where the passenger seat should be. (*Author's note: This pertains to Bundy's August 16, 1975 arrest by Utah Highway Patrol officer, Bob Hayward, in Granger, Utah, greater Salt Lake area, shortly after 2:00 a.m.*)

11:00 hrs. R/O had phone contact with Sandy Gwen who advised that when she knew Bundy that her car was stolen; that on one occasion Bundy drove her all around the "toolies" on the east side of Lake Sammamish. She could not go back to the area as she wasn't paying much attention to where they were. They were in the car and he was driving. She became irritated with his driving around looking for the house of some older lady she thought an aunt or grandmother. There were few houses around, according…

…0830 hrs. R/O had phone contact with Mark Adams, Pedline Surgical Supplies, 17000 Aurora W. He recalled that Bundy worked at Pedline 3 ½ to 4 years ago when his father was managing the place. Adams Sr. has passed away. Mark Jr. worked with Bundy on a part time basis, they would fill orders and deliver merchandise. Bundy would come to work between noon and one and leave at 4 or 5. This was an every weekday type of job. Pedline had plaster of paris as a…

1000 hrs. R/O received copies by mail of Bundy's 1974 purchases at Nordstrom made on his credit card and copies of his statements. R/O had phone contact with Liz Kloepfer that Bundy owned no denim coat, but did have a red ski parka, a trench coat, a black and white tweed coat he didn't wear much, and she recalled he never wore a ski hat. Liz was in Utah in 1974, from July 29th until August 4th. She also remembered that Bundy had his hair cut at Guy's next to the Coffee Corral on 43rd. Prior to July 14, 1974, Bundy had gotten a hair cut that he didn't like, Liz said it didn't look good, and while she was in Utah he had his hair cut again – very short. She also remembered that the day that they all went to the Dungeness Spit was Memorial Day 1974. Liz gave the name of Mark Wallbom as the person who gave the water skiing party at Lake Sammamish in 1974 that Ted attended…R/O then contacted Mark Wallbom by phone and he advised that a friend, Jim Shober, had been with him at Lake Sammamish Park in July 1974 and had already contacted Seattle Police Department, but it was unknown whether they had re-contacted Mr. Shober. Mr. Wallbom specifically remembers seeing Bundy at lake Sammamish the weekend of the State Republican Convention in Richland, Washington. (*Author's note: this would be the 7th of July, exactly one week prior to his double-abduction at the lake the following Sunday. I mention this incident in The Bundy Murders, and one would think that having run into people he knew on the 7th, might have been enough to keep him away from Lake Sammamish the following week, seeing that he could very well be seen and remembered. And yet, Bundy wasn't troubled by such risks.*) He also remembers that this was one week before the Rainier Beer Fest. He and his ex-wife and Jim Shober and wife Tracy were water skiing in the (unreadable) north of the swimming area, where the water skiers go. It was in the later afternoon when they observed Bundy, whom they knew from activities within the Republican party, walking along the beach by himself. They invited him over and Bundy stated he liked the water but either didn't have shorts, or he'd have to get his shorts before joining their activity which he did not do. Wallbom's recollection is that Bundy was wearing a blue t-shirt with a yellow insignia of some type (fraternity) and possibly was wearing long pants. They talked about politics and going water skiing in the future.

File

Det. K. McChesney

Mark believes the day was Sunday rather than Saturday and remembers that the skiers had a chicken dinner that day. Mark was coordinator for King County Youth for Evans in 1972 and in 1973 ran John Spellman's campaign. He was also involved in demographies (*sic*) and as Bundy was also involved/interested in that type of thing they had many conversations in 1973. Either Bundy or Wallbom was involved in Jim Mattingly's campaign around this time. The last time Wallbom saw Bundy was in early June of 1974. Bundy was walking in Red Square at the U, wearing a blue button-down denim shirt, tan khaki pants, penny loafers and a beige fisherman's sweater around his neck. This would have been a weekday as Wallbom was preparing to graduate in the near future (that quarter) and they discussed that. Bundy stated he had been studying at the law library.

Mark remembered distinctly what Bundy said when confronted (*Author's note: "Confronted" seems misplaced here as it was a meeting between friends and/or political co-campaigners*) at Lake Sammamish – "Just walking around." Wallbom thought Ted could be the kind of guy to do that sort of thing, but it was unusual for him to be at Lake Sammamish when he should have been at the Republican Convention or in Tacoma, where his school was.

Wallbom thinks he saw Bundy near the U another time that year but does not recall it clearly. He also saw a lot of Bundy during the 1973 campaigns. Wallbom gave the number of Jim Shober (redacted) and his wife Tracy (redacted). Wallbom was advised that a statement would be taken from him in the next few days…

Phone contact with Mrs. Ferris who stated she knew Bundy and wished to talk with someone in person regarding him.

11:20 hrs. R/O had personal contact with Mrs. Ferris at her residence (*redacted*). Mrs. Ferris is 69 years-old but has a good memory of her dealings with Ted Bundy. She advised that she met him about 5 years ago when he was working as a busboy at the Seattle Yacht Club. Another person that knew him well there is Kenny Gilman, who is now a chef at the Moose Club by the Seattle center. Mrs. Ferris recalled Bundy taking men home who were drunk and other employees suspected him of trying to "roll" the customers after hours. She also remembered a young secretary whom Bundy took up to the "Crows Nest" for sexual purposes. Bundy is a schemer and a sneak according to Mrs. Ferris, and would befriend older people like herself and live with or off of them. He had little or no money and would borrow money and fail to repay it. He would often borrow Mrs. Ferris' car and be gone into the night. Mrs. Ferris later thought Bundy might be robbing but was afraid of him at the time and still is and requests her name not be used. She got Bundy a job at the Olympic Hotel as a busboy and he worked there for a few months as he did at the Yacht Club. Persons at the Yacht Club suspected Bundy of breaking into the employee's lockers and on one occasion he showed Mrs. Ferris a waiter's uniform (new) that he had taken from the Olympic. It was around this time that Bundy borrowed some of Mrs. Ferris' china and silver to put on some special sort of dinner for his girlfriend who was a high-class girl from San Francisco. Bundy had showed Mrs. Ferris how he learned to prepare and serve an excellent dinner to the girl and put on a British accent for Mrs. Ferris. During this time Bundy had borrowed a car from someone but later got a VW from Tacoma which needed a good deal of work.

Bundy also had a job at a Safeway store on Queen Ann Hill stocking shelves at night and he also lived in an apartment on 17th N.E. and then Mrs. Ferris helped him move to an address between 1037 and 1047 on (redacted). This was the home of an elderly couple whom Ted lived with. He met them by knocking on doors around the neighborhood, looking for a place to stay.

Mrs. Ferris remembers about 4 years ago Bundy coming to her house on a rainy day in a grey VW. He had an 8-10-year-old with him and said they were going horseback riding in Issaquah and borrowed an umbrella.

Mrs. Ferris had also an old address of 4127 12th NE #11 for Bundy. phone ME33060. Bundy told Mrs. Ferris his father was a chef.

Several years ago, when Ted was out of the University of Washington, he took a trip to Philadelphia to visit an uncle in politics. Mrs. Ferris took him to the plane and gave him $100 (*Author's note: in 2020 that would be $723*) which she later tried to get back and called Mrs. Bundy looking for Ted. Mrs. Bundy said that Mrs. Ferris was a fool to give Ted that money and she'd never get it back and Ted was a stranger around there. When Ted returned from Philadelphia, Mrs. Ferris took him to the airport again – he was going to Aspen, Colorado to be a ski instructor. Mrs. Ferris was going to knit Ted a ski hat, but he already had one, possibly white, that fit over the face. She also recalled mention of seeing his girlfriend from San Francisco in Aspen.

Bundy had a key to McMahon Hall and sometimes would go inside and sleep when he had no other place to sleep. He went for some time with his girl who attended Stanford and had a desire to go to Taiwan to get out of the army.

Ted also had a friend who lived on Sunnyside Ave. and who owned an antique shop in his home and also worked in a prison. Bundy lived with this man for a while.

Bundy had a black wig that he showed Mrs. Ferris and Mrs. Ferris also saw a picture of him during the Rosellini-Evans campaign wearing a wig.

On one occasion Mrs. Ferris drove Ted to Diane's (the girlfriend's) house on Greenlake (?), and another time she went to the ocean on business and Ted went with her. They also made a trip to Mossyrock and at other times Bundy would take the car to "visit his parents". He borrowed Mrs. Ferris's phone to make a lot of calls.

The last time Mrs. Ferris saw Bundy was in the Post Office on the Ave. before he went to Salt Lake. They had small talk at that time. During the time she knew him best he never talked about going to law school. She also vaguely remembers seeing Ted at the Albertson's store in Greenlake with a cast on his arm.

Mrs. Ferris remembers Ted going to Ellensburg frequently and to meet friends from there to go skiing. He would ski at Snoqualmie Pass or Crystal Mountain. When he went to Aspen, Ted had new, imported ski equipment – something he could not well afford. She has no idea where he got his money and recalls him mentioning he had a strict home life.

Mrs. Ferris took R/O to locate the places she knew Ted lived in. She was unable to locate the address on 17th but will look again and call this office. She also showed R/O Bundy's residence by the Seattle Yacht Club.

1400 hrs. R/O received a phone call from Jim Shober who remembered that on the date he saw Bundy he had a windbreaker thrown over his shoulder. An appointment was made to obtain a written statement from him on October 14, 1975. R/O had phone contact with Susan Reade and requested Republican activity schedule for 1974. She advised that Larry Voshall might have a lot of the information requested and that the only reason she could think of for Bundy to be in Oregon would be to visit Jim Waldo who was with Action for Washington and attending Willamette Law School after campaign of Gov. Evans.

10-12-75 1630 hrs. R/O had phone contact with Marleigh Lang who advised that Diane Zuendt (*Author's note: this would be Diane Edwards, Bundy's former girlfriend who had agreed to marry him a year earlier. Bundy had no intention of marrying her, of course, as he was just trying to pay her back for dumping him earlier in the relationship.*) would be calling her that evening regarding Bundy. Diane works four days per week, is 29 years-old. Marleigh recalled a rich uncle of Bundy's living in Seattle. She also felt Diane was uncomfortable with the relationship – that he couldn't be trusted or figured out. 10-13-75 1100 hrs. R/O had phone contact with Marleigh Lang who said that Diane would be expecting my call on Tuesday evening.

Susan (*Author's note: this would be Susan Reade*) also advised that Rita Butterworth, whose husband is a professor at the UW did the scheduling for the Republican Party that year and may still have those schedules. Often the party would sponsor seminars around the state teaching potential candidates how to run a campaign and Bundy was involved in this but nothing out of state that she knew of. Also, Ross Davis, of the Republican Party, might know about Ted's travels.

1430 hrs. R/O had phone contact Jim Waldo, US Department of Labor (redacted). He did not remember Ted coming to visit him at law school but thought he may have gone to Oregon for some reason with Tim Clancy (former bill reader with the Democratic Caucus at the House of Representatives) or John…who is with the Dept. of Community Development. Waldo considers Ted a pretty good friend and saw him at political and social events in 1972, 73, 74. The last time Waldo saw Bundy was before he went to Utah to law school. Also, any picnics the Republicans had during this time period would have been in northern Seattle.

1530 hrs. R/O had contact with Marleigh Lang, friend of Diane Edwards Zuendt. Diane spent her first year of college at the University of Colorado at Boulder. During 1966 she attended the U. (*Author's note: University of Washington*) and met Bundy and they started dating prior to ski season. During 1973 – 74 Christmas holidays it is likely and possible Bundy and Diane spent New Year's together as they were engaged at the time. Diane was going to return to San Francisco until summertime and then her plans were to return to Seattle and get a job and firm up her plans for marriage. In early September or late August of 1974 Marleigh got a letter from Diane stating she and Ted had broken off and that…had been living with a man for two months. She stated "I escaped by the skin of my teeth" and "when I think of his (Bundy's) cold and calculating manner I shudder."

Marleigh also remembers Diane driving Bundy's car during the summer of 1973. At Christmastime Diane wrote and reported she had married William Zuendt. Mrs. Lang has photographs available of Diane. She intends to call her and advise her that this department will be contacting her regarding Bundy.

10-23-75

O815 hrs. Phone contact with Liz Kloepfer, who advised that Ted's grandparents (last name Cowell) lived in Philadelphia and his grandmother died about a year and a half ago. His grandfather is still alive and living there. John Bundy's parents live in the Ozarks. John Cowell Sr. and his wife live in Arkansas. Liz also stated that John O'Connell, Bundy's attorney said that he might be charged with crimes in Colorado. She remembered the warehouse that John Mueller went to with Ted in west Seattle – this warehouse belonging to Mueller's father's business. In September (early) and late August of 1974 Liz's car was wrecked and she was driving Ted's car as Ted had wrecked hers.

0900 hrs. Phone call received from Nancy Scherer who teaches zoology at the University of British Columbia. She met Ted around July of 1974 at Dept. of Emergency Services. In mid-May of 1975 Nancy, Carol Anderson and Dick Wolf, got tired of Olympia and decided to go skiing in Salt Lake and stayed with Bundy – they told him they were coming…Carol Boone had called and or written Bundy a few times during the past year. Carol had a ten-year-old son. She was also considering going to Salt Lake over Christmas of 1974 – 1975 but didn't for some reason.

While they were in Salt Lake, Ted was nice, she remembered an English Racing Wheel, hanging from the ceiling on a chain and a meat hook similar to a chandelier. Nancy never went out with Bundy alone. The social things they went to were social type things associated with the baseball team. Nancy recalled Ted living with his parents in Seattle, she thought this unusual. After the baseball game they'd drink beer and sometimes Ted would stay all night with Dick and Nancy (*Author's note: this page of the copied record is extremely light at this portion, and I am having to decipher it carefully. Where I can't,, I will insert an ellipsis.*) who lived in the same house. They also gave Ted a key to their house. He stayed about three times. He... stayed at Carol Anderson's house also. Ted would sleep on the couch. There was no physical relationship between Ted and Nancy or Carol or anyone at...

10-24-75 Phone contact with Steve Butler, who is employed by SPD (*Author's note: Seattle Police Department*). He recalled having met Bundy in the winter of 1973 at Fourth and Cherry when Bundy ran into Butler's car. Bundy was driving a VW at the time and he had a white male with him. It occurred at noon or 1:00 p.m. on Saturday or Sunday. Bundy didn't want to go through his insurance company and said he would pay Butler. Butler paid for the damage himself and hounded Bundy for payment ($25) and finally wrote Bundy a letter for the money. There was much damage to Bundy's car a bunched in left bumper and fender in front. Butler will check his records to determine the date of the accident and recontact this office.

0900 hrs. Phone contact with Janet Fisher, ex roommate of Edna Cowell. She lived with Edna at 905 NE 43rd from Sept. of 1973 until June of 1974. Janet graduated in December of 1974 – lived in the apartment alone after Edna moved out in June. She knew Ted Bundy only through Edna - he came over for dinner and drinks on one or two occasions – possibly John Cowell was there. On another occasion - around Christmas or the first of the year Bundy came over and made some hot spiced wine. Ted wasn't the type to drop in. On this occasion Edna, Ted, and Janet went to the Windjammer in Ballard, they all paid in cash. Janet will try and recall the date they went out. Janet never dated Ted socially.

During this time Ted was attending the law school at UPS. (*Author's note: University of Puget Sound*) One time, Edna and Janet went to Ted's apt. looking for him but he was not home. Janet also thinks she may have seen Bundy on the street in the U District but wasn't sure…she recognized him. She did see him out one time near her apartment.

Janet does not know Lynda Healy. During 1973 Edna went to Hawaii for Christmas. Janet has gone places casually with John Cowell. On the night the three of them went to the Windjammer they stopped at a bar right by…met two guys who came back to Edna and Janet's apartment. They played cards or something until 2 or 3 a.m. and the two guys left. Shortly after that Ted left.

Edna has a boyfriend, Don…whom she has been seeing for about 5 years.

10-27-75

0830 hrs. Phone call from Freda Rogers who said she does not keep her phone records after income tax time and that she would not be able to tell which calls belonged to Bundy as all her renters use the phone for long distance. Mrs. Roger's stated she was in poor health and was getting upset because of all the questions regarding Bundy. If she does locate the receipts, she will call this office.

1000 hrs. Phone contact with Liz Kloepfer and arranged to see her the following morning.

Phone contact attempted with Joe McGavick – negative results.

1030 hrs. R/O had phone contact with Steve Butler who advised that he had his car repaired about two weeks after his accident with Bundy which would have made the accident the last of October or the first of November of 1973. The date of the estimate was 11-28. The accident was not reported.

1130 hrs. Phone contact with Pete Neil. Pete works for Metro. His home phone is…He was at Dante's Tavern with Lynda Healy on January 31, 1974. He does not recognize Bundy's photo nor his name. He will call this office if he can think of any connection between Bundy and Healy.

Phone contact with Jake Fry, DES (*Author's note: Department of Emergency Services*) He was the manager of the baseball team for DES and has obtained a copy of the schedule which he is forwarding to this office. There is one game that Bundy definitely attended on July 25th with the Attorney General's Office. The season started on Wednesday, June 26, and all the games after that were played on Wednesdays. Ted didn't show up for all of the games, possibly about 3 or 4 out of the 8 or 9. They played the Attorney General's Office two or three weeks later and it is unknown if Bundy was at that game. There were no practices for the games and all except for the last games were played at ...The last game was played at Timberline High School. The games started around 6:30 p.m. and continued until about 8:30 or 9:00 p.m. Jake recalled going to a tavern after the game a couple of times that Ted Bundy went also. Jake is forwarding notes from the games and any pertinent info, as well as a copy of the schedule of the games (5). There were other games, including playoffs that Ted may have attended on the following weekends.

1300 hrs. Phone contact with Susan Reade. She still has no further information regarding the letter Edna Cowell allegedly wrote to some party in Seattle regarding Lynda Healy. She advised that Sarah Davis, Ross's wife, may have some information regarding Bundy as Bundy used to babysit for her children. Davis's live at 29401 9th Pl. S. Federal Way. Susan is still unable to verify the date of the party she had in March 1974. She also recalled the car that Davis had for the Rep. Central Committee, a white or baby blue Chrysler or some other fancy car. She remembered Bundy working for Art Fletcher's campaign in 1968 through Action for Washington. Jim Waldo may recall this.

10-28-75

1100 hrs. Personal contact with Liz in this office. She recalled Ted's car having primer on the right side and the front. She viewed a photo of the car taken by Salt Lake County and said Ted's car looked browner than it appeared in the photo.

During August of 1973 Ted was driving Liz's car. He got in an accident at 16th NE and NE 52, someone hit him, so Liz used Ted's car on and off while getting hers fixed. She knew that Vortmans had a white VW. She didn't know Ted to drive Ross Davis's car or borrow credit cards from anyone.

She knew about the bicycle wheel in Ted's apartment. He kept it behind his desk and went with him to buy some things for holding it up (chain, meat hook). Also, he had the wheel for approximately one year prior to going to Salt Lake.

Ted talked about doing a report on assaults on women with Liz and went to…to discuss it with someone.

Ted got a ski rack of his own in Christmas of 1974. He did not have a car in 1970, they went to Utah late in August. During the first part of their relationship until August of 1971 Ted spent nearly every night with Liz. After that he only spent a few nights per week with her.

10-29-75

0930 hrs. Phone call received from Detective Barcliff - Thurston County who advised he had made initial contact with Tom Sampson and would be seeing him at 1600 hrs. Sampson stated that after Bundy came to work at DES he used to meet Sampson and they would play racquetball at Evergreen State. Sampson didn't think Bundy was familiar with the college. Sampson also saw Bundy at the…caucus around the middle or the end of February 1974 in the library – Ted was studying.

Sampson recalls the assaults on women project and will attempt to locate a project. Sampson knew Bundy from Seattle Crime Commission and has been drinking with him - dates unknown. Sampson still attends Evergreen State

College. Sampson also has a pamphlet regarding reporting burglaries from the Seattle Crime Commission.

Barcliff thought that possibly Bundy might be involved in some obscene phone calls, as a woman, Mrs. Long, from DES got some obscene phone calls around the time that Bundy was working there and parking his car near hers. Also, Kathy Devine got obscene phone calls from someone with an English accent. They are also checking…records for any record of Bundy being there.

There is also a July 1974 case at Evergreen College of a coed being attacked in the laundry room and her assailant being scared away. Times reporter, Richard Larsen, showed the victim a photograph of Bundy and stated her assailant resembled Bundy.

1100 hrs. Phone contact with Liz Kloepfer who has gone through her personal checks again. She was off work, Monday, March 11, 1974, and Tuesday, March 12, 1974, as Molly, her daughter, was sick. Liz knows she talked to Ted on March 11 as she wrote a check to…newspaper and got the address from Ted. Also, in March she bought some furniture and it was delivered on one of the days Molly was sick. Ted came over and helped her move the furniture, during the day. Liz will check to determine the exact day… the store. (Frederick Wilson – item a wardrobe)

She also believes Ted returned to Seattle on June 6, 1975 for a visit. She thought he shaved his beard on January 20, 1974.

1300 hrs. Requested Liz come to this office for interview.

1400 hrs. Personal contact with Liz Kloepfer, Det. Keppel, Liz Kloepfer, and Captain Mackie this office. Captain Mackie explained to Liz about the ongoing investigation in other states as well as here. Liz recalled that around Christmas of 1973 Ted read "The Joy of Sex" and got some ideas about tying her up and that she agreed when he suggested it. He went to her drawer (she didn't think he knew where she kept her nylons) and tied her up, spread eagle style on the bed with her own nylons. This happened about three times and the third time is when he choked her and she put a stop to it. Also, Bundy's bishop from Salt Lake told Liz that he was extremely depressed by the fact that Liz had contacted the police about him.

1515 hrs. Phone contact from Liz to state that John O'Connell had told her earlier about Ted being investigated in Colorado.

Det. Strunk contacted this office with information that he had that he received a phone call from Pandy Cameron (*Author's note: this would be Pande-Cameron*) rug dealer in Seattle who in July of 1974 had cleaned a rug for Bundy. Det. Strunk will investigate this further.

10-30-75

0810 hrs. Phone contact with Diane Edwards. Diane stated that while Ted was at Stanford for summer school, he stayed in a freshman dorm – she remembers because she visited him here one time. He also came to see her one time that summer, rode his bicycle from Palo Alto to San Mateo, as he had no car. Ted was studying Intensive Chinese at the time. He flew to California initially. During her junior year (before Ted was at summer school) Diane had told Ted she didn't want to see him any longer. This was in the spring of 1967. Diane attended summer school at UW that summer and wrote to Ted at Stanford. She remembered also that on July 8 of that year she turned 21 and went to dinner with Ted in San Francisco. She doesn't remember how this happened as she doesn't think she flew home just for that, although she may have. She did not let Ted use her car at this time.

Diane said that Ted wouldn't accept the fact that she didn't want to see him anymore. He acted like he was falling apart and wouldn't understand. While he was at Stanford, he wrote letters to her regarding this. The reason she broke up with him was because he couldn't be trusted and was so different. Looking back, she feels that the way he treated her in the winter of 1973 was revenge for how she had treated him. At this time, she was ready to use all of her savings to send him to law school – but he lost interest.

When Ted showed up in the fall of 1969 to see Diane in San Fran, he was…try and get her back…he stayed a couple of days but Diane can't recall where he stayed. Ted seemed to want Diane's approval on things. She criticized his manners and lack of confidence on occasion.

Diane is familiar with John Duffy who lives on a boat in San Fran. She will try to locate him or a number for R/O. John was Ted's floor advisor at the UW and didn't care for Ted.

When they first went together Ted and Diane's sexual relationship was tender but markedly different after 1973 when he thought he was a "cool dude" with much more sexual experience. Since the last phone call in 1974 Diane has not heard from or seen Ted.

1000 hrs. Phone contact with Jim Boverman, Hoskins, Oregon. Boverman is good friends of Tim Clancy who is currently in Europe and who also knows Ted Bundy. Boverman has never met Bundy, however, and Bundy, to his knowledge, has never come to Oregon with Clancy. He thought that possibly John Fratt – employment unknown - may know Bundy.

Phone contact with Joe Burnsten, ex-supervisor of King County Law and Justice Planning. He recalled that Bundy worked for him for 3 or 4 months on a part-time basis and thought he was paid by the house. He was doing a paper on the courts and persons in the criminal justice system. Burnsten thought that Chuck Collins might remember Bundy. Bundy was referred by Joe McGavick and paid by research funds from the County Executive's Office. Burnsten describes Ted as bright, articulate, but he didn't finish his work, or receive his last check. Burnsten recalls Ted finishing up his degree.

Bundy was politically active particularly in the Evans campaign and talked about the clever things that he did or that could be done in the campaign. Bundy talked like he was responsible for asking questions that were embarrassing publicly to Rosellini and was involved somehow tripping up Rosellini and was involved somehow in the speech in which Rosellini called Gov. Evans "Danny Boy".

Bundy worked late in the afternoons and sat near a couple of girls. One Asian, one...

11-3-75

Phone call received from Janet Fisher. She was clear on the fact that Ted Bundy was at her and Edna's apartment on two occasions, one time to make hot spiced wine and the other time when they went to the Windjammer. When Bundy was there making the wine it was in the last couple of weeks of October or the first week of November. He had no beard at the time. As best as she can recall the three of them went to the Windjammer on a Friday or Saturday night between December and March, though probably in January.

Phone call from Liz Kloepfer who said she does not wish to be hypnotized.

Phone contact with Jerry Thompson, Salt Lake County S.O. regarding Ted Bundy's phone. On November 21, 1974 at 11:03 p.m. Bundy called... (Louise & Ward Young). At 11:07 p.m. there was a call to Robert Edwards, Diane Edwards father in San Mateo. Thompson will forward a copy of the phone bill to this office.

Message left for Gloria Hamilton at Rainier Bank.

Phone contact attempted with Warren Dodge, negative results.

10:30 hrs. Phone contact with Capt. Ingram, UW Police, will check to see if another subpoena needed for UW law school records pertaining to Bundy. Ingram advised he would call back.

Phone contact was attempted with Ivan Weiss – negative results.

(Author's note: After Bundy's second arrest and the subsequent search of his apartment at 565 First Avenue, Detective Jerry Thompson found a brochure that had obvious meaning to the investigation, and it clearly made Bundy nervous. Before presenting an interesting entry from the record pertaining to this, it is appropriate to add that portion from my book, The Bundy Murders: A Comprehensive History, to set the scene that will add substance to what the record is revealing. We pick up where Bundy is seated on the sofa with deputies guarding him, and Thompson begins finding items Bundy realizes might end up connecting him to the murders of Caryn Campbell and Debra Kent.)

"The items of interest Bernardo and Thompson would find were "a book called 'The Joy of Sex,' a road map of the state of Colorado, a Colorado Ski Country Guide '74 and '75, a brochure from the Bountiful Recreation Center, a copy of a Chevron gasoline bill listed to Theodore R. Bundy, and also a copy of a phone bill for the month of June, which listed a telephone call to Denver, Colorado.

This was odd indeed, as Detective Thompson had asked Bundy early in the search if he'd ever been to Colorado, and he had said no. When asked if he had any friends in the state, or knew anyone there, he answered no to this too. Having found the Colorado items, Thompson walked over and inquired of Bundy if he could keep them, and Bundy, never one to object, looked up at the stern-faced cop and said it "would be no problem." But Jerry Thompson wasn't about to let this promising suspect off so easily. He would do a little probing too.

Addressing his seated suspect, the detective asked about the Colorado maps and guides. "They were left here,"

Bundy responded, "by a friend of mine who was talking about how good the skiing was over there." When quizzed about the brochure from Bountiful, he feigned geographical ignorance and answered: "Is that the city just north of Salt Lake? I've heard about it, and probably driven through it, but I've never been there to speak of." The smiling, nervous, and talkative Theodore Bundy was lying, and Jerry Thompson knew it.

Pressing him further about the brochure (which was in fact an advertisement for the Viewmont High School play), he said that "a friend of mine ... left it there, some kid of his or something that went up there to some kind of deal." Bundy's use of words at this point is little more than grammatical mumbo-jumbo, so it may signal that he was experiencing a higher degree of anxiety. That would certainly be something he'd attempt to conceal from Thompson.

0915 hrs. Phone call from Liz Kloepfer – she thought that the brochure that Ted had in his apartment may have come from Richard Bundy when Richard was visiting Salt Lake in August. Mrs. Bundy took Richard swimming in Bountiful and they could have picked up the brochure at that time. Liz also inquired as to why the Salt Lake authorities had not previously shown a photograph of Bundy to the victim in their case as she had turned him in in October of last year..."

0930 hrs. Phone contact with Warren Dodge, childhood friend of Bundy's. The last contact Warren had with Ted was about 2 years ago. Around the time Bundy graduated from the UW. Bundy was working for the Republican Party at the time, so it might have been prior to 1973, Dodge says.

During their first year in college Bundy and Dodge had more contacts. Dodge was at Olympic J and UPS (*Author's note: University of Puget Sound*). In 1967, Dodge recalls Ted dropping out of the UW and go skiing and to visit relatives in Philadelphia. Dodge thinks Bundy was gone about five months. He remembers Bundy taking his skis with him but doesn't know where he skied at. After 1968 or 1969 Dodge didn't have much contact with Bundy. Around this time Ted returned to the UW and talked about a girl (Author's note: I believe Bundy was seeing) with Warren.

When they were kids Ted would hang around Dodge's house and therefore Dodge didn't know Bundy's folks well. He describes Mr. Bundy as a weak father figure, who was strict. Dodge didn't know Ted's relatives. Dodge describes Ted as intelligent, shy, not aggressive. He didn't have many relationships with girls in high school...

Mr. Bundy was a scout leader for a while. The kids later went camping at the ocean a few times but Ted never went. Dodge said that Bundy got along well with the rest of the kids in his family, as he was older, he did have to babysit a lot. Ted often didn't have money but didn't make a point of it...On occasions Mr. Bundy would hit Ted with a belt, Dodge didn't know the reasons...Other persons who know Bundy are Terry Storwick...Ken Kessler...Bundy's scout leader was R. Cook, who is a shop teacher at Hunt Junior High in Tacoma. Warren described John Bundy as...not much of a father figure. Bundy was primarily responsible for raising the kids.

11-13-75 0830 hrs. Phone call from Ed Hoeing, Standard Oil. He advised that he thinks that possibly the difference Salt Lake City received the same information from them as we did, he thinks that possibly the difference in our accounts are clerical. It was learned that one page was missing from our credit slip – purchases on 5-16 in Seattle, 5-15 in Tacoma, and 5-30 in Seattle. He will recopy the information from the microfilm and forward to this office.

0930 hrs. Phone call received from Mary Grandee... she heard from Don Martin, Edna Cowell's boyfriend, that he had received a letter from Edna indicating her concern about Ted Bundy and Lynda Healy being possibly acquainted.

This was about one month ago that Mary talked to Don, who is a good friend of hers.

1400 hrs. R/O attempted to locate the address 109 S. 5th in Tacoma which is the alleged address of Ted Bundy's sister, Linda. This particular address does not exist and R/O then made phone contact with her. Linda was very upset and very hostile towards R/O and did not want R/O coming to her home. She said that she cannot pin down any dates she might have been with her brother, she said "I never saw my brother." She also stated that her parents had already spoken with police and she saw no reason to talk with them also.

Phone contact with Mrs. Ferris who advised that the antique dealer Ted lived with in 1968 was living and working out of a large, two story house west of Phinney Ave.; possibly Greenwood Ave. This man drove a VW van.

She also recalled that the people that Ted lived with near the Seattle Yacht Club were an older couple who were going to go to Norway on a trip and let him live in the house for them but then decided against it. They were an older couple. Mrs. Ferris thought that Ted was at their residence most of the summer of 1968 and then she helped him move back into the boarding house on 16th NE.

0900 hrs. R/O and Det. Dunn had general contact with Marlin Vortman, 1200 IBM Building. Marlin advised he would attempt to determine if he was with Bundy on any of the dates the girls in the area went missing. He also talked about the fact that Ted was seriously considering marrying both Diane and Liz in the fall of 1973 and this produced a great conflict for him.

Vortman also thought Bundy was having some sort of conflict with law school and implied Bundy wasn't really buckling down. Vortman has known Ted since 1972 and the last time he saw Ted in 1974 was when he helped Ted load his truck to move to Salt Lake.

Vortman commented that he thought that the items found in Bundy's car in Salt Lake were indicative of a burglary and he thought Bundy had pantyhose with holes in it for skiing.

11-18-75 (*Author's note: the beginning of this copied report is extremely light and is undecipherable. We pick up this report on the following page as a continuation.*) Rita described Ted as cooperative, reliable and dependable. She also talked with Liz Kloepfer on the phone. She described Ted as interested in party politics. His duties were to compile briefing data on communities for the governor but he was not an advance man. He did phone and library research. He also monitored the opposition. He put together the candidate's fair at Seattle Community College and monitored the fair.

Rita did not know Ross Davis until this year – she said specific campaigns were not associated with the party a great deal. Rita heard of (*indecipherable*) 1968 when he put together a successful doorbell campaign in…She also recommended Ted to a job that Joe McGavick had.

The only place that Ted went out of town on the campaign for…was the time he took the ferry to Port Orchard and was accused of following Rosellini with a tape recorder.

Rita recalled that Ted had some other activity or job or school during the campaign.

11-19-75 (*Author's note: The beginning of this report is missing, and we pick up on what is the second page.*) …any medical records. He thought that perhaps, Brenda Alexander who was the medical secretary at the time would know about that. Or perhaps Dr. Lunnaberg.

1640 hrs. Phone call received from Liz Kloepfer who said that Peyton Whitely had visited her and said she had told him she had no comment to make.

Liz recalled taking Frieda Rogers to Sky Nursery to buy some garden seeds and also to buy a plant for his mother.

Liz visited a guy named Richard who owned the Daily Planet, an antique store in the U District. Richard went to jail for stealing antiques and one-time Ted and Liz visited Richard's girlfriend while Richard was in jail.

Richard has had other antique stores and one-time Ted used to live with Richard in a really neat house that was filled with antiques.

CHAPTER TWO

TESTIMONIES

I received the following letter in 2010 from a friend who was skiing at Snowmass on the same day that Caryn Campbell was abducted by Ted Bundy on January 12, 1975, and in fact, he continued to ski there for the rest of the week. It should also be said he was an accomplished skier who was very familiar with all the slopes and knew the area well. As can be expected, when he learned what had happened to the nurse from Michigan, it sparked an interest in the case that has lasted for many years now. So, for a look into the past by someone who was there, here is his letter. Because I believe my friend would like to retain his anonymity, I have not used his name and the letter is only slightly redacted.

Kevin,

Please find a Snowmass trail map from the 78-79 season. The map was in with some photos I had of my '75 trip, but it's from a couple of seasons after '75.

The Wildwood Inn is in that cluster of lodges to the right of lift # 1 on the map. I flew into Aspen that week on January 11. I had a great flight connection and was skiing down the runs serviced by the lodges peak lift on Aspen Highlands by 2pm. The next day, I skied Snowmass. While Ray Gadowski (Author's note: this is Dr. Ray Gadowski, the boyfriend of Caryn Campbell) was ducking out on his

Dr's conferences, I was skiing over on Elk Camp and then hitting the runs on the Big Burn for the afternoon. I skied from first lift until last run, when they would always have to shoo me off the mountain. Around, 5:30, I would have passed right by the Wildwood, taking Fanny Hill at the bottom of the mountain, skiing to the bus stop to catch the bus into Aspen.

I skied Snowmass, Aspen Highlands, and Ajax the rest of the week. Rumors and tales of the missing woman at Snowmass began to filter out over the backyard telegraph after a bit. At some point, the local rags (*Author's note: slang for newspapers*) printed a story about Caryn Campbell's disappearance. The papers usually held off on stuff like that, 'cause Ray Gadowski wouldn't be the first doctor to lose his girlfriend to some wild local boy in Aspen. When she didn't turn up and it was obvious foul play might well be the reason, there was a different buzz in the old rumor mill. Ray Gadowski was tried, hung, and convicted in the local gossip court…

Then, over the years, I would be out there reading Bundy stories when I went skiing in Aspen again. I was out there when his trial started, when he escaped, etc. That coupled with the fact that Bundy went to Florida when I was there fishing and diving during his murder trial give you a pretty good idea of my interest in the case.

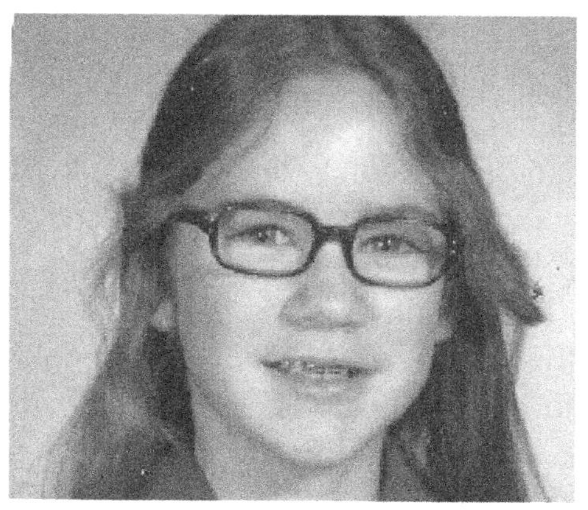

Michele Komen, who was stopped by Bundy one morning while walking to her bus

Bundy abruptly turned into this driveway, and attempted to convince Michele Komen to get into his car

MICHELE KOMEN NELSON

Michele Komen Nelson was a young junior high school student when, early one morning, she had an encounter with a man that both she and I believe was Ted Bundy. Her father, John Komen was a newsman in Seattle and in his long career has worked for KOMO, ABC, KING, and the

Tacoma News Tribune. Without question, she was very fortunate she didn't fall victim to the killer, and I'm happy to include her story here. Michele starts out with a brief statement, and then it follows a normal Q&A between us.

I lived in North Seattle and was in junior high school at the time. I was walking to the bus stop and a man in a VW passed by me a couple times. He then turned into a driveway blocking my path. He asked for directions to the high school, said he didn't understand, why didn't I get in the car and show him, and he would take me to school after. The front seat was missing in the car, my bus was coming, I told him to follow the bus. I ran to the bus, hopped on and he didn't follow the bus.

Q: Do you remember approximately what year and what month this happened?

A: I am thinking it was either fall-winter of either 1974 or 75. My brother went to Ingraham High School; I went to Thompson Junior High. We could walk to Northgate Mall and we shopped at the Bon Marche that he stole the TV from.

Q: Yeah, I remember the TV theft story but forgot what store Bundy hit. As to Bundy, do you remember what color was the VW? Thanks for trying to remember these things. Very often, thinking along these lines can spark memories. Like, did the VW have any noticeable dents or blemishes? Anything about him? His clothes, was he wearing a jacket? Do you remember what his hair looked like?

A: It was in the morning and it was light out. No cars on the streets. Not raining. The car passed me twice then turned into a driveway blocking my way. I went around the car--it was a light-colored VW bug (remember TB had his own and used Liz's and his friend's VWs, too). A good-looking young man rolled down his window and called me over asking if I could tell him how to get to Ingraham High School. This was a white man with curly brown hair, a nice smile, average build, and a little flirtatious. I remember that he had dark eyes. (TB had blue eyes, but I later read several times that his eyes would go dark in hunting situations.) I remember thinking he was handsome and I was flattered that he would ask me because, after all, I was just a junior high school kid. I tried giving him directions. He said things like he didn't understand, he couldn't hear me, etc. Then he suggested that I show him. I said I couldn't as I had to get to school. He said it was no problem because he would take me to school afterwards. I remember looking in the car. Something was wrong with the passenger door and the front seat was missing -- which meant in my young mind that I would have to sit in the back. My mom's friend had a VW slug bug and from experience I knew the back seat was not comfortable and I also was a bit claustrophobic. My heart started beating really hard. He was very cute and persuasive--it was no problem; I could do this, he would take me to school, I wouldn't be late, etc. I was thinking of ways to get away, nicely of course, because that is what females are socialized to do. I began looking around. I said that he could follow the bus because it went right by the high school--that would work. I looked up across the top of the VW and saw my bus coming down the street. I said here comes my bus, turned heel, and ran to the bus stop. I went towards the back of the bus, I asked someone if a VW was following us. They said no. I think I wiped a window to look and, of course, no VW. He was off. I didn't put two and two together until much later in life. I knew a college woman had disappeared, but she was a WOMAN and so much older. In fact, I remember going to a hardware store at the mall with my parents. I read the Sunday paper while they were shopping and the big story was the missing girls. (My dad was a journalist and I read both the Seattle papers.) I didn't connect the dots at the time. The older I get, the scarier this encounter becomes. He was all over my neighborhood from the mall to the cemetery to the hospital to Hwy 99.

Dad's name is John Komen. He had a fantastic career working for KOMO, ABC, KING, and the *Tacoma News Tribune*. He knew Dick Larsen, can't remember the name of the Trib writer who knew TB. Norm Heffron was a news director for KING TV and if memory serves me, his daughter knew either Healey or Hawkins.

When Michele mentioned the front passenger seat was missing, she also said the passenger door didn't look right. When I asked her about this, she said:

With the door, it was just wrong and registered with me. It could have been missing a crank or panel or something.

CHERI RANES

This is the story of Cheri Ranes and her sisters, who believe they had an encounter with Ted Bundy. After reading her communication, my original thought was it was an interesting story, but given the factors of the white van, as well as some other possible issues, I decided to put it aside. However, months later I was speaking to a fellow who has followed the Bundy case for years, and he happened to mention to me one day that there have been some stories circulating that Bundy may have been using a white van on occasion when he was involved with murder while in Washington State.

When I first heard this, I remembered Cheri's story and began considering the possibilities. Of course, I'm aware Bundy made deliveries for Ped Line Medical Services for a number on months, and I wondered if they might have had a white van? And even if this wasn't the case, it is also well–known that Bundy, throughout his life, would occasionally borrow the vehicles of friends and acquaintances, and it was more common than most people think. And it was because of the mention by others that Bundy may have used a white van that I'm including this story in the book. Was it Ted Bundy who came calling that day? We do not know. Who was the person who followed her home from the drive-in? Again, we don't know. But because Cheri and her family lived in Bellevue, Washington during the same time period when Bundy was geographically close by, we can at least wonder about it, just as I wonder about the white van. Again, it's a strange story, Bundy or not.

Hi Mr. Sullivan. I've been wanting to know for some time what kind of vehicle Ted Bundy drove around 1969-1970. It seems that you would be a good person to reach out to about this. Specifically, did he own or have access to a white van? I'm asking because I believe my sisters and I had an encounter with him when I was 15 years old. When Ted spoke of failed attempts from that time period, he was referring to me. We've never talked publicly (and barely privately) about this, but it's a missing piece from his early days. The incident so terrified us that we didn't speak of it for many years. I was his primary target and I'm ready to talk to someone about it now. I believe my 5 sisters are too. At least some of them. Do you have any advice for me? Thanks.

Aside from a counselor and a few people close to me, I haven't talked to anyone about this. I'll give you some details. We pretty much repressed the memory for a long time. My 5 sisters and I were home with one or two friends while our parents were on vacation. We lived in Bellevue, a suburb of Seattle. They had just left that morning for Mexico. It was, I believe, 1970 (possibly over our spring break) and our ages at the time ranged from around 17 to 5 years of age. I was 15, almost 16. It was still light outside although sunset was approaching. The 4 older sisters, myself included, and our friend were in the kitchen talking and laughing when there was a knock at our front door (maybe doorbell). My two youngest sisters (around 7 and 5) were tumbling around in the living room, close to the door. We yelled out to them not to answer the door as we walked into the living room. However, they had already opened the door and the man immediately pushed past them and was a few steps inside our home. He never asked if our parents were home. He obviously knew they weren't. He pretended to be a telephone repairman and said he was there to repair our phone. We told him there was nothing wrong with our phone and we didn't request service. He said that one of our friends probably requested service after being unable to get through.

I remember we were all trying to process what he was saying. It was like he was reading a rehearsed script. The front door had been left open and he pointed to his vehicle, which was a white van with no windows in the back. The van was parked on the side of the road in front of our house. It seemed strange he didn't drive up our driveway like everyone else always did. It was like he was using the van to try to convince us he was really from the phone company. Also, he was wearing white overalls that looked new. Like he had just purchased them to try to look the part. He then suggested that we check our phone to see if it worked. He pointed toward our kitchen like he already knew where our phone was located. We walked into the kitchen with him, lifted up the phone and there was no dial tone. He then looked directly at me and said he needed to see our fuse box. I told him he would need to go outside and enter the basement from the side of our house to find the fuse box. There was no way to access the basement from inside. But I think he already knew that too.

He then asked me to go outside with him to show him the way. I told him okay and followed him to the back door. He walked out the door and I pretended like I was going to go with him. I quickly shut and locked the door and we all immediately dispersed and made sure all the doors and windows were locked. The man walked around our house outside yelling to us to let him back in. He was looking through our windows at us and laughing. We all (except my older sister Debbie) grabbed a weapon of some sort (knives, fireplace poker, etc.) and locked ourselves in a bathroom. We put our younger sisters in the bathtub and told them to keep the shower curtain closed so they couldn't see and made a plan that if he tried to get in the door or bathroom window, we were going to use our weapons on him. Debbie, in the meantime, ran to the other end of the home.

My dad owned his own business for which he had a separate business phone line. Thankfully that phone line had not been tampered with and she was able to call a friend of my parents who lived about 2 miles away. She also contacted the phone company and was told they did not send a repairman to our house. She ran to our location and joined us in the bathroom where we waited, hoping family friend (Eldon) would get there before the man broke in. We could still hear him outside talking loudly to us. He seemed to be enjoying the fact that we were so freaked out. Eventually we heard a vehicle drive up our driveway. Eldon exited his car and we could hear him yell at the man who took off running to his car. He drove away very quickly.

Why do I strongly believe it was Ted? A few years later when I saw him on television for the first time, I told my mom he looked just like him. The age, thick wavy brown hair, shape of face, size, all matched. For years I wondered why us? How did we come to his attention? Then a few years ago when I started to do some more in depth reading about him, it hit me. I read about him being obsessed with pornography. At age 15 I was working at a drive-in theatre near Seattle that started to show X-rated movies. I believe I came in contact with him there and he followed me home and stalked me for some time. Our home was on a few acres with lots of woods and places to hide. Several things happened to me around that time that I thought were unrelated but now I wonder. I won't get into that because this is already so long. He put a lot of time and effort into planning. He used a ruse to attempt to lure me away from my sisters. I had long straight brown hair parted down the middle. I would like to be hypnotized to try to remember certain things. My sisters, at least some of them, may want to also. One last thing. My sister, Jeri, and I hung out at Lake Sammamish Park and were there with a group of friends the day the two girls went missing from the park. Sorry this is so long. There's more I could say but I'll save that for another time.

ROBERT STOTT

Robert Stott was a part of the Salt Lake County prosecution team headed up by David Yocom that presented the case against Ted Bundy for the abduction of Carol DaRonch. During my research period for my book, *The Bundy Murders*, I had the opportunity to interview by phone both David Yocom and Robert Stott, and both men were very helpful and willing to share their experiences; many of which I have written about in the book. And for this book, I have pulled some emails out of my files for this book, and what Mr. Stott sent me carries some interesting anecdotes about Bundy and the case he'd ultimately lose. Lastly, my dealings with Bob Stott occurred in 2006 and 2007, and at that time, he was still a prosecutor in Salt Lake City.

From Robert Stott…

I have some vivid memories of that trial in the old and small, but most judicial-like courtroom. I believe that it was the first trial in our jurisdiction in which those wishing to view the trial were required to pass through a metal detector. It was not because anyone feared that somehow Bundy would receive outside aid, but because of the concern that one of the fathers or supporters of the missing girls would attempt to kill Bundy in the courtroom. Bundy and Yocom soon got on each other's nerves. Because it was a trial to the Court, and not to a jury, things were more relaxed and informal. In fact, the judge allowed Bundy to ask questions and to make some arguments. Dave Yocom, being Dave Yocom, was aggressive and sarcastic with Bundy. Bundy would get back at Yocom by calling him "Dave." This, in turn, incited Yocom to become even more aggressive and sarcastic. Soon, through clenched teeth, the words "Dave" and "Ted" were thrown back and forth at each other.

The most amazing aspect of the case was the way in which Bundy daily changed his attitude, demeanor, and even appearance. The court room was very narrow and as a consequence the two council tables were right next to each other. To separate Bundy and Yocom, I sat on the outside of our table next to the defense table within two feet of Bundy. One day he would come to court looking and acting like Joe College. He would wear a blazer and stripe tie with penny loafers. Completely shaved and clean, even glowing, he was the epitome of helpfulness and courtesy. It was "yes sir" and "no sir" and "how may I help you." The very next day he came to court looking like a gangster right off the street. He had, what appeared to be, a three-day beard with unruly and uncombed hair. He looked greasy and wore a wrinkled tee shirt and Levies. He was surly, talked back to everyone, and was completely uncooperative, even with his attorneys. Then, on the third day, he was suddenly a wall-street attorney, complete with a briefcase, three-piece suit, spit polished shoes, short hair and a white, buttoned-down shirt. He tried to take charge, even to the point of wanting to do the cross examination of the witnesses and addressing the court as a lawyer. I had never, and have never, seen anyone who had the ability to overnight so completely change their personality and appearance as Bundy did during those days of the trial. One last thought, final arguments ended on Friday afternoon, I believe, and the judge announced that he would think about the matter over the week-end and bring back a verdict on Monday. Yocom leaned over to me and said that when the judge returned home over the weekend and saw his two teenage daughters, he would return with a guilty verdict.

Susan Milner, after having a disagreement with her husband, was asked by Ted Bundy to take a ride with him

SUSAN MILNER

People contact me on a regular basis, from all over the United States, and other countries as well. Sometimes folks just want to tell me how much they like my books, and I always appreciate their kind words. But sometimes they contact me with a story to tell. And such is the case with Susan Milner, who could have easily had a fatal encounter with Bundy after they crossed paths in Salt Lake City, Utah. Here is her story in her own words.

Warm greetings, Kevin!

Thanks for taking the time to respond to my Facebook message. The following is my little experience with the monster, Ted Bundy…

My fiancé and I left Georgia and went to Utah to be married in the Provo Temple of the Church of Jesus Christ of Latter-Day Saints. We were married on September 10th,

1974. My husband got a job at Zion's Bank and we moved into a little apartment in the Avenues of Salt Lake City. The apartment was situated on the second floor of the building over top of the E Street Pharmacy, a little corner pharmacy and soda fountain shop where I worked.

The day I met Ted Bundy:

About mid-day, my new husband and I had quarreled. It was a mild day. I left the apartment, walked to the corner and headed west, toward Temple Square/downtown area. As I walked down the sidewalk, I came upon a school... possibly an elementary school, because it had a swingset sitting within a fenced-in schoolyard. The swingset faced the street. I had a strong feeling that I should go inside that school yard and sit on the swing. However, the only gate I could see was way down the side of the school yard, much closer to the building. I started to simply pass the swing, but again, had a strong feeling to go inside the fence. So, I backtracked, walked down the side of the fence, went inside the gate and walked up to sit on one of the swings facing the street. I sat there pouting for a while, thinking of the quarrel between my husband and I. And then a yellow Volkswagen drove up and parked along the curb.

A good-looking man got out and came to the fence. He smiled at me and leaned his forearms along the top of the fence. At the time I had no idea who he was. I think he said, "Hi," though I'm not quite sure how much small talk took place. He asked me if I wanted to go for a ride. I immediately turned him down. After all, I was newly married. I was mad at my husband but certainly not mad enough to go off with someone else. He seemed agitated. He asked me again to go for a ride with him and I turned him down again. He seemed angry for just a second and then calmed. He patted his fist softly against the top of the fence a few times, shook his head, walked back to his car and drove away.

It was years later that I saw Bundy on TV and told my husband, "Hey, that is the guy that asked me to go for a ride with him." It was only then that I realized how close I came to my demise. I often think that if I hadn't had that urge to go inside that fence, who knows? I think he couldn't think of a way to get me over that fence and decided he'd have to look elsewhere for his prey. If I'd merely been walking down the sidewalk, he may have been able to get me. I don't remember exactly what month it was. It was very early into our marriage. I was pregnant but not showing yet, so I'm thinking the very end of September or early October of 1974.

My first husband, Terry Clements, passed away in 2013. But we have 7 children who've heard this story many times. My name at the time was Susan Clements. I would turn 20 years old at the end of October 1974. Thanks for your time and the opportunity to tell my little story. Let me know if you have any questions.

Susan Milner

I then followed it up with the email below:

Hi Susan

Thanks for the story, and yes, that may very well have been Ted Bundy. A small point: his VW was beige and not yellow, but these kinds of things can sometimes get changed around in our minds over time. Anyway, I'll keep your story, and if I have any additional questions, I'm assuming I can contact you.

Thanks again,

Kevin

Susan then responded...

Funny about the color of his VW. I've seen a few of these documentaries where they've said it was beige and I would tell my husband... no.... it was yellow. I've also seen a few of the documentaries where they say or perhaps portray it as yellow. I distinctly remember it as yellow... a pale yellow, but I guess I could be wrong. However, the man I remember. I didn't see him again until I saw him on television and I immediately recognized him. Take care and wishing you great success!

Sincerely,

Susan Milner

Scott Brainerd, one of the ESAR kids, searched for the remains of Bundy's victims on Taylor Mountain

SCOTT BRAINERD

The following information comes from Scott Brainerd. As a youth, he was a part of Explorer Search and Rescue (ESAR) and he participated in the search for human remains on Taylor Mountain, and if you've ever been to Taylor Mountain or have seen pictures of the thick underbrush there, you'll appreciate his story. He goes into great detail about ESAR and what a contribution they made, not just at Taylor Mountain, but throughout the state of Washington. And I specifically asked Scott if he could give us background information on ESAR, as very little is known about it by the general public. And yet, anyone who has read my book, *The Bundy Murders*, or Bob Keppel's books on the Bundy case, know something about the work of ESAR during that tough week on Taylor Mountain. But what you read here will widen your perspective on why these dedicated young people have accomplished so much. I know it did mine.

I was born in Tacoma, Washington, in December 1957. I grew up in Lakewood, which at that time was an unincorporated suburb of Tacoma, south of town, near Steilacoom. My father worked for the Washington Department of Highways and was heavily involved in the construction of I5 between Tacoma and Olympia in the early 1960's. He was also in the Seabees as a reservist, where he served for 25 years. He retired from the Navy in 1972, when he was an instructor at LH Bates Voc-Tech, teaching highway construction technicians. He was president of ASCET, the American Society of Certified Engineering Technicians, in the 1970's. He traveled extensively between the Seabees and ASCET during that time around the country. I grew up in a patriotic, conservative family. We had an oversized flagpole that was a radio mast from the mothballed USS Hornet (CV-12) in our front yard, and I raised and lowered a big ship's flag every day during the Vietnam War. Our house got egged on more than one occasion because of that! I was in the Boy Scouts, and achieved the rank of Eagle Scout in 1973. I was in Troop 51 based at St. Mary's Episcopal Church across from Clover Park High School in Lakewood. I wore my uniform on uniform day at school and remember that was pretty unpopular at the time. The Vietnam War was raging at the time. I worked as a volunteer on a Washington Game Department facility, the South Tacoma Game Farm, during 1971-1975, and recall young Vietnam vets coming back to work with us as part of a transition to civilian life. Some of their stories made a powerful impression on me.

My tenure in the boy scouts gave me the skills I need to thrive under sometimes challenging conditions year-round. After many years in the boy scouts, where I eventually became a Junior Assistant Scoutmaster, I wanted to move on to something more challenging. I determined to join ESAR as I wanted to perform community service and improve my outdoor survival and rescue skills. I was frankly bored with the boy scouts and wanted real world experience and to apply my knowledge and abilities in a useful context. Oddly, I thought, my father and the scout leaders were initially not supportive of my choice, but I persevered.

Explorer Search and Rescue is and was an elite organization with an arduous and challenging training program designed to recruit the most motivated and skilled young people for real world SAR missions. It was open to both girls and boys, and this was particularly attractive to me as a 16-year old! I underwent training in the winter of 1974-75, which consisted of four tough weekends where we were pushed hard. I recall getting kicked out of my tent (a boot to the head!) at two AM to do a simulated rescue of a hypothermic victim, carrying him to safety from a remote cabin along a snowy, muddy and slippery trail on a rescue litter. That was tough work that took several hours to complete. In the end, we were told that he died and that our effort wasn't good enough! My arms must have become about two inches longer, even though we rotated through the line every couple of minutes. Later, I would have a similar, exhilarating real life experience carrying a litter down a steep mountain in a human chain with several hundred other rescuers from PC and KC ESAR, near Mount Erie. That time, the victim survived and was flown to Whidbey Island NAS in a Navy Chinook helicopter. I helped load the litter onto the helicopter, which was filmed by a Navy crewman wearing a gold flight helmet.

We also had to pass a strenuous orienteering course and winter avalanche rescue training and camping on the slopes of Mount Rainier in February 1975. We were required to take a long course in Advanced First Aid, taught by Shorty Williams, in downtown Tacoma. That course served me well in later life. I renewed my certification regularly through the years. I actually had to perform CPR on a person in Oslo, Norway, once, successfully, and he can owe his life to my previous training.

While I was in training, Pierce County ESAR and other units from western Washington made the news when they were involved in the dramatic rescue of some lost hunters near Spokane. It was a two-week, intensive search in the middle of a winter snowstorm. The National Guard was called in. Embarrassingly, the NG also got lost, so ESAR had to go and rescue the NG and the hunters. I think about a dozen hypothermic guardsmen and the hunters were rescued. Pretty humiliating for the guard, but it gave ESAR a real boost. ESAR was airlifted to Spokane by the Air National Guard in C-141 Starlifters. Pretty exciting for those involved. I really wished I could have been on that mission. I was very proud when I officially became a "brush monkey" (as we proudly called ourselves) in March 1975 and received my Civil Defense ID card. I was active in ESAR during 1975 and 1976 until I graduated from Lakes and moved to Alaska in September 1976. I had flirted with the idea of going into Mountain Rescue, which was really the most elite volunteer SAR unit in the state, but ultimately did not. Some of my ESAR colleagues were also in Mountain Rescue, and two of them were killed during that time in mountaineering accidents. I think that put me off a bit.

The history of ESAR in Washington State, where it all started, is intriguing and deserves its own book. We worked closely with local authorities, including the military (army and navy, national guard), and different law enforcement units, including Pierce, Thurston and King County Sheriffs offices, Washington State Patrol, Tacoma city police, etc. I do not recall any interaction directly with Bob Keppel, but I likely saw him at Taylor Mountain as we interacted a lot with LE there.

One thing that was attractive about ESAR to a young teen like me was that we were on call 24/7 and had to have our backpacks packed and ready to go for a 48-hour search. My backpack was always ready to go in the corner of my room. I had a driver's license and a '63 VW bug so I could be out of the house within 20 minutes of getting the call. My parents were supportive, even though they didn't always appreciate the 2am calls! Getting off schools for up to a week at a time was also attractive! It made me feel important and useful.

I attended Lakes High School (1973-1976). This was at the height of the Bundy rampage in western Washington. Georgeann Hawkins had graduated the spring previous to my sophomore year, so I did not know her personally. But many at school did, and we were all shocked at her disappearance. It was in the news constantly, as more girls disappeared. I remember being really enraged by it all.

One of my first missions in ESAR was the Taylor Mountain search, in March 1975. While in ESAR, I participated in a number of searches for murder victims, lost elderly people or children, evidence searches for the Sheriff's department, etc. Sometimes we found the victims (as we called them) alive and well, sometimes they were deceased. One committed suicide while we were searching for him. That was rather frightening as we were told he was armed and dangerous and to not approach him! Some of my colleagues had some hair-raising stories, particularly relative to recovering plane wreck victims. I am rather glad I did not participate in those. For a 17-year-old boy, it was an awakening in many ways.

As stated, the kidnappings and murders were all over the media during that time. They were called the "Ted" murders because it somehow became known that his first name was Ted. There were composite sketches from near-victims that were used in the manhunt to find him shown in the media. Since our high school had been directly affected through the disappearance of Miss Hawkins, it hit very close to home. UW was miles away in Seattle, but we were directly affected because of this, even those like me that did not know her personally. We were a pretty big school, about 2000 students. I graduated in 1976 in a class of over 750 students. We were in a military area – Fort Lewis and McChord AFB, so many of the kids were from military families, active and retired. It was a great community and place to grow up. Bucolic, and thus in great contrast to the murderous rampage of Ted Bundy, which unsettled us all.

The search on Taylor Mountain was like something out of a gothic movie, however. I struggle to recall all the details 45 years later. We assembled somewhere in town before sunrise and drove to the site in a 1952 vintage green Chevy bus that ESAR used. I believe I spent the entire week on the mountain. I cannot recall details of camping or provisioning. I think we were fed with warm food, army style, but I cannot recall now. I think we just camped out in our pup tents on site. All I remember is it was so gloomy on the mountain that we needed flashlights to examine possible remains because it was so dark in the woods where we were searching. We crawled shoulder to shoulder through the woods, line abreast. PC ESAR was there in strength, as well as King County ESAR and other county units. I was told there were 400 of us in the line as we crept along for hours digging through the forest humus looking for remains. We wore thick rubber gloves with wool mittens inside, as well as wool clothing, stocking caps hats under our plastic helmets, heavy hiking boots and rain gear. It was cold and rainy, dank and dark. Every few minutes the line would halt, and the sheriff's office personnel (possibly coroner) would move down the line to collect and photograph whatever was found. They had big format cameras with flashbulbs. You could see sometimes the flash of the bulb down the line when they were documenting something. We cleaned the woods of many old animal bones and a huge pile of women's clothing and shoes that I was told was completely unrelated to the Bundy murderers. A lot of pornography was also strewn around in the woods. It really made me wonder about the state of humanity in this tranquil area. I mean that pile of clothes and shoes was monumental. It was probably 6 feet high and 20 feet at the base. I wish I had a picture of it. It was really creepy.

We were all in a very somber mood on Taylor Mountain. It was foggy, dark, and raining the whole time. The forest was dark and had an oppressive feel to it. There was some gallows humor among some of my colleagues, something I found a bit offensive. But we were all trying to cope in our own way. I recall a local news team tried to interview me. They had a camera right in my face as I was getting out of my tent in the morning. I just ignored them. I didn't relish being interviewed, although some others enjoyed it. We all knew we were part of something big. Momentous. And frightening. I remember lying awake at night in my tent and contemplating the fate of those young women. It was just horrible and unimaginable to a young guy like me. We kind of lost some of our innocence on Taylor Mountain. It was cold, exhausting and depressing work.

I dug up some bones that we determined were probably from a coyote, but it was just a few fragments and no skull. A mammal but not human. I did not find any human remains. I was rather relieved that I did not. Others did. I believe two skulls were found on that search, but I am unsure now. We were all heavily impacted by the circumstances. The search went on for weeks so it might have happened before or after I was there. I believe I was there for about a week.

I recall being away from school for a week. I have some photos from that time, taken with an instamatic camera. They are very dark, almost too underexposed to see what is going on. The pictures reflect the somber and gloomy mood, however.

Back then, we used Motorola VHF portable radios with whip antennas. They were heavy to carry. We received extensive radio communications training. Added a lot of noise and a sense of urgency to the missions. We had a big mobile radio communication unit that accompanied our searches. They would coordinate us as we often couldn't communicate directly with each other due to topography. Also, they would redirect us if we needed to shift the search or come in once the search was resolved.

We had heavy 50-pound overnight framed backpacks and carried big daypacks with first aid and survival gear. Later I underwent Assistant Team Leader training and became an ATL; but only served on a few more searches before I dropped out and moved to Alaska. Later, in Alaska, there was little interest in ESAR. Most searchers at the time were conducted by air, usually for lost aircraft. Later, some citizen units were formed, using dogs to look for lost hunters or hikers. I tried to start an ESAR unit in Fairbanks but didn't get a positive response from scout leaders there and dropped it. A few years ago, a search got lost near Fairbanks and was never found.

CHAPTER THREE

ODDS & ENDS

Did One Watch the Other Die?

Janice Ott, Denise Naslund, and the
Lake Sammamish Murders

Because I have discussed the murders of Denise Naslund and Janice Ott at Lake Sammamish in great detail in my previous Bundy books, I will only be focusing on one aspect of the crime that remains a mystery to this day: where did he keep Janice Ott (who was abducted in the morning of July 14, 1974) while he returned to the park to convince Denise Naslund to leave with him as well. But because of a current controversy (did Bundy actually kill one woman in front of the other?) concerning what I consider established fact, I'll be delving into that as well.

It is unknown by this writer how many cabins, abandoned or otherwise, are in the area close to where the remains were discovered on September 7, 1974. But one thing I do know is that no location was ever identified by the authorities as being a suspected location he might have used to house her, and nothing supports Bundy using a cabin at all, but it's still possible he did. In any event, I don't believe we'll ever know for sure where it all transpired other than to say he had them well away from humanity. That said, I will tell you what I have personally believed for many years now: Bundy likely kept Janice bound, gagged, and tied to a tree while he went back to the lake for another victim. It wasn't a theory I shared very often as it was partial speculation; partial, because if he didn't have them ensconced in a cabin, then there aren't a lot of other choices. But beyond the logistics of why Bundy did whatever he did, pertaining to where he kept them, I think the idea of Bundy securing Ott to a tree where (even though the chances were likely small) she might be discovered, is the kind of "reckless" thing Bundy enjoyed doing. That Bundy loved to take chances is without dispute – Lake Sammamish proved this!

And then, earlier this year, I received a phone call from a friend who is also heavily immersed in the Bundy case, producing documentaries and currently writing a book. And he mentioned the possibility that Bundy had tied Ott to a tree; something I immediately agreed with and told him my long-standing theory about it. I did not tell him that I also suspected Bundy may have gotten that idea from one of the numerous detective magazines of that time that often featured on the cover cowering, frightened women, bound and gagged with a menacing man (or men) standing over her with a knife or some other weapon in his hand. Without question, they were creepy magazine covers, and it was Bundy's favorite magazine. The domination and fear he saw in these women were a turn on for him. And from the looks of these covers, it appears the women would not be escaping their captors. It's no wonder Bundy, with his fractured personality, found them so stimulating. In any event, my friend alluded to this very thing, hinting there is such a cover on one of the detective magazines, and while it doesn't "prove" anything, it does bolster my belief that Bundy kept all his activities in the open air that day.

Now, another aspect that needs addressing is an issue relating to the deaths of Janice Ott and Denise Naslund that some believe are a bit unclear, and that's whether Bundy kept Janice Ott alive and brought Denise Naslund to where he had secured her? If true, it was a most horrendous and horrifying thing to do with the two women, as one would have to watch the murder of the other knowing she was next. And apparently, that's exactly what happened, as I state in my book, *The Bundy Murders*. What follows is from the volume *Serial Killers*, part of *Time-Life Books* series, *True Crime*: "*...Also, Bundy confirmed for Hagmaier a horror that other investigators had long suspected: On the day he kidnapped Janice Ott and Denise Naslund from Lake Sammamish, he kept both alive for a while. One had to watch the other die.*"

But while Bundy confirmed to Bill Hagmaier that he did, in fact, keep Ott alive and that Naslund and Ott saw each other (which means that one was killed in front of the other), Bundy also gave great detail about these murders years earlier while talking to Stephen Michaud in the third-person. What follows is from his book, *Conversations with a Killer:*

SM: Would the second victim see the first victim?

TB: Oh yeah, probably. In all probability.

SM: Would the other individual still be alive, or not?

TB: Well, had he been cautious, he would've probably killed the first individual before leaving to get the second girl, but in this instance since we've agreed he wasn't acting cautiously, he hadn't killed the first girl when he abducted the second.

SM: Would there have been any unique thrill or excitement from having the two of them there together?

TB: In all probability we're talking about an aberration here, a unique circumstance.

SM: Would the first victim be conscious?

TB: In all probability.

SM: What happened when they encountered each other?

TB: It seems there would be little importance attached to the arrival of the second individual. It seems the person would be more acutely interested in her own welfare and well-being.

I suppose if you took two such individuals and kept them confined for days or months, they would certainly establish a rapport and be very concerned about each other's welfare. Here there was a good amount of fear and panic—most of us freeze under those circumstances.

We might surmise that in this case there was little interaction, as such. This individual would not want any interaction, as he did not want interaction on a one-to-one basis.

SM: What happens then?

TB: He'd follow the same pattern with the second girl as the first.

SM: In view of the other girl?

TB: In all probability, yes.

SM: After the sexual assault, he has two bound victims. What does he do now?

TB: Well, by this time his frenzied compulsive activity of that day has run its course. Then he realized the jeopardy he was in. Then the normal self would begin to reemerge and, realizing the greater danger involved, would suffer panic and begin to think of ways to conceal the acts—or at least his part of them. So he'd kill the two girls, place them in his car, and take them to a secluded area and leave them.

SM: Right away?

TB: Within a matter of hours.

(*Author's note: This would mean that after Bundy took Liz and her daughter for hamburgers and ice cream, Bundy went back to where he had left them, and transported them to where they were later found, as it's likely he wouldn't have waited until the next day. Of course, that's something we'll never know.*)

Lastly, during my writing of *The Bundy Murders,* I interviewed Bill Hagmaier twice by phone. Having already read this information in *Time-Life Books* and *Conversation with a Killer*, I never brought it up as I already had his statement about this terrible event. However, in the years since and as these questions have surfaced, I phoned a friend who speaks with Bill Hagmaier on a regular basis, and I asked him if Bill ever confirmed this story to him. He said yes, Bill did confirm it, and coupled with the two examples above, as far as I'm concerned, that settles the question for all time.

Did Ted Bundy Use the Money of His Dead Victims?

In my many years of writing about Ted Bundy I have never covered this topic in any of my books, and for two reasons. First, it's an area of speculation, and in dealing with the absolute facts of Ted Bundy and the case, first my biography of Ted Bundy, *The Bundy Murders: A Comprehensive History*, and then later in my three companion volumes: *The Trail of Ted Bundy: Digging Up the Untold Stories; The Bundy Secrets: Hidden Files on America's Worst Serial Killer*; *Ted Bundy's Murderous Mysteries: The Many Victims of America's Most Infamous Serial Killer;* and lastly in my encyclopedia of the case: *The Encyclopedia of the Ted Bundy Murders*, I felt that delving too deeply into speculation, would best be left to a future volume of the case, where many speculations could be addressed. And that time is now, here with this book.

A number of months ago, I tested the waters of my theory on a Facebook post. I felt a good example of where Bundy might have benefited from the cash of his victims was at Lake Sammamish State Park in Washington State. For it was here, on a hot July 14, 1974 Sunday, that Ted Bundy abducted two women from the park that had some 40,000 people enjoying themselves from early that morning until late afternoon. It was both risky and foolish, since he could run into someone he knew (as he had the week before), but that didn't seem to bother him. Indeed, it appears that Bundy was rather perceptive when it came to the dangers of being apprehended, and throughout his career of murder, he learned to navigate those waters (unfortunately) very well. At no time during these years of murder did Ted Bundy ever come close to being captured, except when he was caught in the women's dormitory at Idaho State University in Pocatello, Idaho. True, Bundy would leave damning hints of himself at Lake Sammamish, but that would not really come back to haunt him until his unveiling in Utah.

Anyway, the monies Bundy would have gotten ahold of during the abductions of Janice Ott (in the morning) and Denise Naslund (in the late afternoon), would not have been thrown away. Bundy would have kept it. How do I know this? Well, first of all, Bundy worked only sporadically and was always in need of money. Not only this, but he was constantly receiving financial help by the women around him—first and foremost, his main girlfriend, Liz Kendall, who was helping him pay for law school. Not only that, but after they met in September of 1969, Bundy, over the course of the next few years, would spend a great deal of time with Liz at her place, and it's not much of a leap to posit that, while there, Liz paid for almost everything. Add to this, Bundy's girlfriends he accumulated over the years he was with Liz, and the money they spent on him, it becomes quite clear that Bundy lived near poverty when he wasn't working. And because Bundy had become over the years both a bold and an efficient thief, he was able to fill his apartments wherever he went with the stolen possessions of others. This is how Bundy lived his life, and he was perfectly content with it.

And so, when I presented my theory on Facebook that Bundy "must" have kept the money of his victims, most fully understood my reasons for thinking so, and a number added that it was an aspect that they'd never thought about or considered, yet it all made sense. There were one or two detractors, of course, but the reason they gave for rejecting the theory did make a great deal of sense. That being said, let us look a bit deeper at the nature of Ted Bundy, and let's see if there are any "signs" or indications that he wouldn't have kept the cash of the women he killed...

Beyond the pocketing of the cash due to his dire financial state, let's look at his nature, and in fact, the nature for all humans, for that matter: Keep in mind, when you have someone like Bundy who thinks nothing of stealing lives and destroying families forever, and then add that he lives a life of also stealing cash, credit cards, and what other items he can lay his hands upon to snatch, we must come to the undeniable determination that whenever Bundy encountered money on his victims, and this would almost certainly include the change they carried, leaving it there or even burying it, would be inconsistent with every other action ever taken by him. No, the truth of the matter is, while he was never a direct robber of people, and he certainly didn't abduct women for purposes of monetary gain, Bundy did consider the money on his victims an unexpected gain, and he would make use of it.

As to Lake Sammamish, we will never know how much money, if any, he took off of his victims, Janice Ott and Denise Naslund. Nor can we know what monies were obtained during each encounter. But in some of his cases without question, the women would have had cash on them. In the case of Lake Sammamish, I think we can say the following: Because Denise Naslund had left her purse in her car, it's likely she had no money with her as Bundy led her away to the parking lot. Sure, she could have had a few bucks stuffed in her bra, as many women have admitted to doing, but that is just speculation. However, when Janice Ott left the park with Bundy that morning, she had her bike with her and most likely had some cash on her too. And if this is the case, then when Bundy went out with Liz and her daughter Molly for hamburgers and ice cream later that night, it was possibly courtesy of the money earned by Janice Ott.

Carol DaRonch vs "Today's" Bundy "survivors"

Because this book tackles questions, controversies, and the answers where we can find them, I'd like to make some observations about recent "survivors" of Bundy that have come forward over the last decade or so, to tell their stories. First, when someone comes forward for the first time, 20, 30, even 40 years after an event, proclaiming they were a part of the Bundy story, they will (and should) be met with a high degree of skepticism. And then, even if down the road we do come away from it thinking a particular story *might* be true, the fact remains that because they never contacted the police as other women did, we can never know for sure. As such, many will believe it, and just as many won't. The passing of 30 years can never add credibility to the story. Also, there are many false claims out there that are very easily proved false because their "story" occurred in a geographic area and span of time that rules Bundy completely out of the picture. And unfortunately, even when women contact me, and I am able to provide all the proof they would need to rule Bundy out, invariably, they refuse to do so. It's like they want the connection to Bundy, as it makes them a part of the story. And that alone can tell you a great deal about human nature.

I must also say that I occasionally see women pop up on television or in news stories, with their tale of escape from Ted Bundy. And of course, I'll begin taking mental notes as to why it is either highly unlikely it was Bundy, to absolutely it couldn't have been him. And in no time (and maybe this is new in journalism, and if so, it certainly is not an improvement), the media seems to just take it all in, and just believe every word that comes out of their mouths. On my end, I'm listening to what they said Bundy said, and I'm saying in my head, "Oh, no he didn't; he would never give himself away like that; he would have never said something so stupid."

Another will have him 1500 miles away from where he was known to be at the time (one lady had him attacking her in Louisville, Ky, my home town, in 1974, at a time when he was busy killing in Washington State), but in their mind, "It was Bundy!". And on exceedingly rare occasions, I will hear of an incident that happened in an area where Bundy was operating and at the time he was operating; and coupled with other things they said occurred, I will come away from it thinking (in some cases) it's a high probability they encountered him, and in others, yes, it was no doubt Bundy.

But for these women with their wild and completely unprovable stories, even if they are true, at no time can we put them in the same category as Carol DaRonch, as Carol went straight to the cops after Bundy attacked her, and cooperated with the authorities. This led to Bundy being convicted of her abduction, leading to his incarceration in the Utah State Prison. And that is why I can say with confidence that Carol DaRonch will remain, no matter what other stories you'll hear, the only verifiable female to ever escape from Ted Bundy.

Bundy's rooming house at 565 First Ave. in Salt Lake City, Utah; it was here where Bundy "housed" some of his victims

Did Bundy Keep Living Victims in His Room?

Of all the controversies surrounding the Bundy case, this one might be at the top of the list, at least when it comes to drawing the mocking and the ire of those who do not believe it. So, this will be a good place to tackle this occasionally debated question about Bundy and some of his Utah murders.

When I was writing *The Bundy Murders: A Comprehensive History*, I had the pleasure of working with many people who knew Bundy and many of the lead detectives who hunted him, including Michael J. Fisher, the Colorado investigator who was involved in the case for 15 years, and who obtained the first murder warrant against the killer. And it would be Mike who first presented the idea to me that both Melissa Smith and Laura Ann Aime may have been kept at Bundy's 565 First Avenue apartment in Utah. The reason he believed this has to do with the times of abduction for each victim and the approximate times of death for each. As such, it became clear to him that Bundy had them alive somewhere for a number of days, and his apartment seemed the likely place.

In the case of Melissa Smith, she was abducted on the evening of October 18, 1974, and would not be discovered until the afternoon of October 27th. After viewing the body, however, it was determined that her death had probably occurred no more than 36 hours prior to the discovery of her body. That means she was alive, and perhaps in a comatose state for perhaps 5 or 6 days. In the case of Laura Ann Amie, she was abducted around midnight on Halloween night, but would not be discovered until Thanksgiving Day, November 27, 1974. In this case, we're looking at almost an entire month since she disappeared, and yet, when found, her body was not showing signs of decomposition (I've viewed the crime scene photos, and there appears to be no decay present at all). And it wasn't the temperature keeping her body frozen, as it rarely drops below freezing during November in Utah. So, it's clear to me that he most likely had Smith and Aime up at his apartment for an undetermined amount of time. It can't be proven, of course, but there's a great deal of circumstantial evidence that points to him using his apartment (there were two possible locations there) as the place where he sequestered his living, but no doubt comatose, victims for a time before murdering them.

And so, in my book, I posit that while it can't be proven, it's likely Bundy had them in his upstairs # 2 apartment. And as I say in one of my previous Bundy books, think of it as a Lynda Healy abduction in reverse: Bundy carried out Healy in the middle of the night in a university district where he could easily have been seen, and got away with it.

So too, he could have carried them up in the middle of the night (it would have taken him under a minute to actually get her out of the car and up the steps if he parked in the driveway, and would have done it the same way when he wanted to get rid of the body.)

And of course, besides my speculation that he had them in his apartment, I knew of what he told Stephen Michaud as he was talking about *his* crimes in the third-person. To give you an idea of how likely this scenario is to the truth, here's a passage from *Confessions of a Killer*:

SM: There's perhaps a lack of sophistication on my part. Having to go in and out of residences with any large bundle would seem to be risking everything, no matter what time of day...

TB: This person taking bundles in, in and out of his house or his apartment. We say in retrospect, that was really chancy. But there were times when I think he... he almost felt as if he were immune from detection.

Not in a mystical or a spiritual sense or anything, but that on occasion he felt like he could walk through doors. He didn't feel like he was, uh, invisible or anything like that. But at times he felt that no matter how much he fucked up, nothing could go wrong.

The boldness was probably a result of not being rational. Of just being moved by a situation—not really thinking it out clearly, and not even seeing risks. But just overcome by that boldness and desire to accomplish a particular thing. Only in retrospect would he wonder how he managed to succeed in spite of some of those rash and bold acts.

Add to this that in Bundy's final confession, he admitted to Utah Detective Dennis Couch that he took Debra Kent up to "his apartment". All of this points to victims coming to 565 First Avenue. However, a number of years after my book was published, I learned that there was, in the rear of the apartment, a cellar with a locked cover to which Bundy had a key. He had the key as he was the acting apartment manager; showing apartments to college kids looking to rent a room, as well as cutting the grass and similar chores. Anyway, a former resident who knew Bundy told how Bundy would go down at all hours of the night and he would hear him moving around down there. As such, we can say that without question, he must have used this for at least some of his victims. After all, he kept Debra Kent only one day, and this would be the perfect place to keep her. During the Couch/Bundy interview, Bundy also admitted bringing young Nancy Wilcox here for one day as well; so this cellar makes perfect sense. And yet, given what he told Michaud, would he have kept Melissa Smith in that cellar for up to six or seven days; and Aime perhaps for longer? I personally doubt it. In my mind, he used both locations, and in all cases, took them in the dead of night far away to dispose of the remains.

So, in the final analysis (at least a final analysis for me), Bundy had victims in his upstairs # 2 apartment, as well as that underground cellar.

When Ted Bundy's Eyes Alerted His Victims

On the outside, Ted Bundy almost always displayed a good character, and it seemed everybody (or almost everybody) liked him. And as killers are wont to do, especially when (he, she, they) are handsome and naturally women were attracted to them, to use that to his advantage when it came to hunting and slaughtering women. And yet, it was clear that one thing he couldn't do flawlessly, is learn to control what happens to his eyes once he felt like a victim was about to fall into his hands. And no, I'm not referring to his greatly depleted mental and emotional makeup in Florida when women found him repulsive in the dance club known as Sherrod's in Tallahassee. No, we're talking about when he was the absolute best at murder, and that would be in Washington State. What follows is a portion of the official records, pertaining to Bundy's hunting activities at Central Washington State College in April 1974. What follows is from the official transcript of the interview of Jane Curtis, an almost-victim of Ted Bundy at CWSC after she saw Bundy, with an arm in a sling, struggling to carry some books, and Jane, being both nice and normal, agreed to help him. I'll first add her response to the detective when she encountered Bundy, and what had changed after she was helping him to his car.

DETECTIVE: What did you do after you left the library?

JANE: After I finished work, I walked out the main entrance of the library, and was just minding my own business, I walked straight out, and I was approached ... well, there was this guy coming along and he had this huge stack of books, like about 8 or 9 books, and he had a cast on his left arm as I recalled later ... but he was carrying these books and all of a sudden he kind of drops them, right in the direction that I was walking in, so I just more or less ... offered assistance. I said, "Gee, well it looks like you have quite a load, would you like some help? So I helped him pick up the books ... no big deal, 'cause he didn't act like, uh, he acted like a very nice person. So I said, "Do you need any help?" He said that he could, so I ... he just happened to be walking in the same direction I was, so I thought it was no big deal if I helped him carry his books out to the car, 'cause the parking lot ... they usually park right behind the library which is just like across, or not even a block away, so I just more or less just helped him carry his books. We went past Black Hall and I was on his right-hand side, and he was on the left, and I remember he was shorter than I was, because I was wearing kinda high shoes, it gave me a couple inches, it made me about 5'9". I remember he was shorter than I..

DETECTIVE: How about glasses?

JANE: ... that's the thing that's been bothering me ... I've been thinking about that. He kind of looked at me sideways

... kind of turned his head and looked at me kind of funny like. He looked at me strangely. His eyes seemed weird...

Notice, at no time as she was talking with Bundy, did she see anything in his eyes that disturbed her. They were no doubt clear and friendly looking; but certainly nothing that would have given Jane Curtis pause. And yet, as they walked between the library, which was to their right, and Black Hall to their left, and were about to enter what was likely the most deserted area on campus where Bundy had parked under a railroad trestle bounded by high grass with little light illuminating them, she turns to look at Bundy who was slightly to her rear and to the left, his eyes had completely changed.

That got me to thinking, and so I contacted Dr. Al Carlisle, the psychologist who evaluated Bundy in 1976 after he was convicted for the kidnapping of Carol DaRonch, and I asked him about it. He responded this way in a September 11, 2006 email:

Regarding his eyes, I have had other women tell me about the eyes of the person about to attack them. There is a difference which is likely due to some form of temporary neurotransmitter changes when a person is in that state of mind.

So, it seems clear to me that Bundy was quickly entering that altered state of murder that only his victims saw, just before their own demise. They say our eyes are the windows to our souls, and I suppose that's especially true about the killers of women.

Did Bundy Murder Two Women in New Jersey?

Part of this, of course, is Bundy's fault. He never came completely clean on everyone he killed. He admitted to killing eleven in Washington State but only owned up to eight by name. Same thing in Utah. He admitted to eight but gave the names of five. Very often, obfuscation was Bundy's middle name.

Because we know Bundy murdered two 12-year-old girls, Lynette Culver of Pocatello, Idaho and Kimberly Leach of Lake City, Florida, and because he made a comment in the third-person killing a half dozen young girls, this may be why he refused to name them. That said, it may very well be there are more adult women he killed that he's never touched upon. In the end it will likely remain a mystery as to the exact number, and who these victims were. Even so, we will continue to speculate.

And what drives speculation in the Bundy case has to do with where was Ted Bundy when such and such women disappeared? And if the victim went missing at a time and location where Bundy was operating at the time he was operating, then it will at that point become (or should become) a matter of inquiry to either rule Bundy in or out of the case in question. And such is the ongoing search to find a correlation, or a connection, that can point to Bundy being responsible. And such is the case for what is known as the Garden State Parkway Murders.

On Memorial Day in 1969, Susan Davis and Elizabeth Perry, were on their way home after a several-days' vacation in Ocean City, New Jersey, where they enjoyed soaking up the sun, eating out, and just having a great time. Both 19, Susan had just graduated from Monticello Junior College in Godfrey, Illinois (near St. Louis), and Elizabeth had a year to go. They had no idea their lives were going to come to an abrupt end as they traveled along the Garden State Parkway. What follows is from Christian Barth's definitive account of these murders, *The Garden State Parkway Murders: A Cold Case Mystery*:

This is the true story of the unsolved murders of Elizabeth Perry and Susan Davis, college friends who were brutally knifed to death during the early morning hours of May 30,

1969, in the woods between mileposts 31.8 and 31.9 of the Garden State Parkway near Ocean City, New Jersey.

Because Bundy continues to be associated with their deaths, I have asked Christian Barth to answer some questions for this book. What follows is a Q&A from July 2020:

Q: What drew you to write *The Garden State Parkway Murders*?

A: The standard answer I give interviewers whenever they pose this question, is this: When I was a boy, about 12 or 13 years old, I was seated in the backseat of my parents car when I heard my mother say to my father, 'They never found out who killed those girls, did they?' just as we were driving past the Ocean City exit on the northbound side of Garden State Parkway, near milepost 31.9. I was immediately intrigued, as obviously I was just discovering my nascent fascination with unsolved crimes. Years later I read an article where Bundy biographer Richard Larsen was quoted as saying that the murders of Susan Davis and Elizabeth Perry were, in his opinion, 'Bundy's first, unplanned murders,' before he further developed his signature modus operandi. This realization—that one of the world's most prolific serial killers was here, at the Jersey Shore, and might have murdered two women near where I'd vacationed every summer since I was a toddler—became the genesis of a short story I wrote titled 'The Smiling Knife.' From there, I decided to write a fictionalized version—almost a true novel, if you will—titled 'The Origins of Infamy,' which was the story of the 1969 Garden State Parkway murders, told entirely from Bundy's viewpoint in 1969, beginning with the fall that year and encompassing Seattle, Philadelphia, New York City, and ending up at the Jersey Shore.

But the story of my continuing fascination with the 1969 Garden State Parkway murders actually predates my initial boyhood memory, as my parents actually first met at a restaurant called Maynard's, about 100 yards from the Somers Point Diner, the last place that parkway murder victims Susan Davis and Elizabeth Perry were seen alive before they were murdered in the woods beside the parkway some 45 minutes after they'd eaten, on May 30, 1969. Whenever I would stop to think about these bizarre coincidences, and stop to consider the eerie parallels the case has with my own existence on this Earth, I would become more and more intrigued, as though the Lord had placed this coincidence before me, challenging me to solve the case. I took it as a compliment when Mark Thomas, one of the Perry-Davis murder suspects I interviewed, told me "you're obsessed with this case."

Q: We know that Bundy has been a suspect in these murders, but there are other suspects as well. After having written what I consider the definitive account of these murders, where does Bundy fall in the list of suspects, and in your opinion, could he be the killer?

A: I don't know that I can actually rate, in order of possible culpability, the suspects in the murders of Susan Davis and Elizabeth Perry. There's certainly a fair amount of circumstantial evidence pointing toward a handful of viable suspects in the 1969 parkway murders, including Ted Bundy. You and I have discussed, with some humorous references, the morass of Bundy "experts" on the internet who cavalierly dismiss Bundy as a suspect in the parkway murders based upon a circumspect denial he made in the hours before his execution, in which he said he didn't kill anyone in New Jersey. These naysayers—none of whom knew of Bundy's familial connection to Ocean City prior to the release of *The Garden State Parkway Murders*—invariably reference a remark he made to Dr. Dorothy Lewis the day before his execution, when he claimed he didn't kill anybody in Ocean City in 1969, but had 'attempted to abduct a woman' in the downtown area of Ocean City, and she'd escaped. (Bundy also referenced his involvement in the 1969 Perry-Davis murders in 1986, when speaking in the third person to another psychologist, Art Norman.) What I learned while researching Bundy's possible involvement in the 1969 parkway slaying is this: Bundy had in fact visited Ocean City, New Jersey, several times over the years while growing up, for his maternal grandparents, according to my interview with Audrey, had a vacation home on 26th Street. Why didn't Bundy delve further into his several previous visits to Ocean City when he was a boy, while speaking with his psychologists during his interview with Dr. Norman in 1986, and his penultimate interview with Dr. Lewis in 1989? Why did he instead choose to discuss on both occasions, without solicitation, the spring of 1969, the season and year when Perry and Davis were killed? Was he baiting Dr. Norman and Dr. Lewis, hoping to buy some time with these vague though oddly coincidental reveries? In my book, I include a picture of Ted at about 4 years old, with his mother and Sam Cowell, sitting on the beach near the 14th Street Fishing Pier in Ocean City. And why didn't Dr. Lewis know more about this part of Ted's familial connection to Ocean City? Collectively, Bundy's omissions regarding Ocean City, and his reference to the spring of 1969, are quite revealing. I think Ted killed a lot more women than we give him credit for. He simply withheld the names of many more victims at the end because he ran out of time or had simply forgotten several of his victims. Moreover, he was rushed, stressed, confused, and heavily medicated. To the extent that serial killers tend to familiarize themselves with their hunting grounds, given his numerous visits to Ocean City, obviously Bundy had ample opportunity to scope out his hunting grounds near the side of the milepost 31.9.

Q: I know from reading your book that you had contact with Bundy's aunt, Audrey Tilden. Can you tell us what that was like? Even though she's in her 90s, does she carry any noticeable scars from what happened with Ted?

A: I spoke with Audrey for about two hours in total, on two separate occasions. A genuinely delightful, forthright Christian woman. What immediately struck me was how genuinely saddened she was, and how sorry she felt, for Ted's victims, and the victims' families. She made this a point of emphasis from the outset of our conversation, and her remarks were heartfelt and sincere. I think it's natural for us to draw certain stereotypes about serial killers and how they were raised, based on what we read and see on TV—dirt poor, immersed in horrid, squalid environments rife with dysfunction and abuse, both physical and psychological. This wasn't the case with Ted's family, especially Audrey. From the first moment I spoke with her, I was almost taken aback by how horrible she still felt, all these years later, about the tragedies that befell so many families, and the unspeakable anguish they would forever suffer, because of Ted.

Q: As you may know, Samuel Cowell, Bundy's grandfather, has taken a beating from many who study this case because of the endless speculations about Bundy's "true" paternity, and Sam Cowell's reported propensity for outbursts of anger, as well as the often repeated story that Bundy found his grandfather's stash of pornographic magazines; something I find a bit odd seeing that Bundy left Philadelphia at a very young age. What's your take on all of this?

A: The allegations concerning Samuel Cowell, Ted's maternal grandfather originated with the testimony of Dr. Dorothy Lewis at a Florida hearing concerning his competency to stand trial. Dr. Lewis had testified that she'd interviewed a number of Sam Cowell's daughters (Audrey was among them) and learned that Sam Cowell had allegedly "swung cats by the tail," and was an "abusive alcoholic" who "threw his daughters down the stairs if they missed curfew." Regarding the allegations that Cowell was an alcoholic: I interviewed a local historian of sorts who'd had many dealings with Sam over the years, as he was a well-known local gardener who had a booth at the annual Philadelphia Flower Show and often gave talks at the local Roxborough (Pa.) Flower Club. She portrayed Sam as a generous, extremely nice man who selflessly donated his time and planting expertise, and had actually planted a dogwood on her lot (the dogwood is there today). Couldn't find a bad word to say about him. Audrey portrayed her father in similar terms, saying she never saw him take a sip of alcohol in his life. She said he taught Sunday school at the first Congregational Church in Germantown, Pa., a church founded by his father in law's family. I've read some speculation that Ted Bundy was a product of incest, more specifically, the love child of his mother, Louise Cowell, and grandfather Sam. This is untrue. Ted's father was John Worthington, whose identity Ann Rule correctly referenced in *The Stranger Beside Me*. I confirmed this with Audrey. In my extensive genealogical research into this matter, which I set forth in great detail in *The Garden State Parkway Murders: A Cold Case Mystery,* I learned of the existence of three John Worthington's living in the Philadelphia area in 1946, the year Ted was born, who were possible suitors. I couldn't confirm, however, which of these three was in fact Ted's father. I feel safe in concluding that he was in fact one of these three men, and was about 30 years old when Ted was born.

Q: Did you run into any opposition while researching this book, either from surviving members of Bundy's family or anyone else?

A: My conversations with Bundy's Aunt Audrey, with whom Ted Bundy lived while attending Temple University in Philadelphia in the winter and spring of 1969—consistent with his latter remarks that he'd visited Ocean City at around the time of the murders—were very pleasant. I also interviewed one of Bundy's cousins from Seattle, and she was very cordial toward me as well. The only pushback I encountered was from a younger sister of one of the 1969 Garden State Parkway victims. This was just after *The Origins of Infamy* was released. This person wrote that she was very upset that I'd disrupted what closure she'd obtained, she said, when the New Jersey state police informed her that Ted Bundy had murdered her sister. Other than that, only one retired New Jersey State Police detective was less than pleasant toward me when I attempted to interview him about his work on the 1969 Garden State Parkway Murder investigation.

Q: Finally, do you believe there is any information "out there", perhaps through future DNA testing or some other avenue of evidence, that will lead us to the actual killer? Is there anything on the investigative horizon that gives you hope the case will finally be solved?

A: Several years ago, I spoke with a detective with the New Jersey State Police Major Crime Unit. He indicated that several years prior, his department had received some cold case funding, and that the Perry-Davis file was among those submitted for DNA analysis. When I asked him what, if any, new evidence had been discovered, he replied, "We have nothing." As to what information is out there, I certainly hope that the New Jersey State Police and Atlantic County Prosecutor's Office review the findings in my book, especially in light of the revelations regarding Bundy's time in Ocean City, the fact that serial killer Gerald Stano who signed a confession to the 1969 Parkway slayings, lived one mile from suspect Mark Thomas, and the two allegedly knew one another when they were teens growing up outside Philadelphia.

Ted Bundy's murder kit on the author's dining room table, May 2005

Ted Bundy's Murder Kit

Anyone who's read my book, *The Bundy Murders: A Comprehensive History*, knows what a part Ted Bundy's murder kit played in my decision to write the book. For those of you who haven't read the book—yet!—here's what I wrote about the profound effect it had on me having these implements of murder in my hands for a few hours.

To set the scene, I was introduced to retired detective Jerry Thompson—the lead investigator for the Bundy case in Utah—by my friend Jim Massie (See his story in the next chapter), and I had already been told by Jim a few years earlier Jerry's role in the case; and in fact, it was in Utah where Bundy was pulled out of the shadows and introduced to the world for the killer he was. Jim had also told me that Jerry had Bundy's murder kit, which Bundy forever lost after his arrest there, and that he used to use it in law enforcement teaching seminars. Anyway, in March 2005, Jim called me and said the Thompsons were coming to Louisville in May, and would I like to have dinner with them. Of course, I jumped at the chance, as I know Jerry was an interesting guy who was involved with one of the most infamous cases this nation has ever seen. What we didn't know was that when Jerry arrived in Louisville, he brought Ted Bundy's murder kit with him. And so, when Jim called me to tell me where we'd be eating that night, he informed me the murder kit was here too:

When the Thompsons arrived in Louisville on the afternoon of May 29, 2005, Jim called to tell me where we'd be having dinner and when. No sooner had I said, "Great" than he interrupted me by saying, "He brought the bag..."

"What bag?" I asked.

"The bag Bundy carried.... I have it with me now in my truck!"

I couldn't believe what I was hearing. I remembered Jim telling me years ago how, as lead investigator for the Bundy case, Jerry had gained possession of the bag and its contents after Bundy was arrested in the Salt Lake suburb of Granger, Utah, in 1975. And then, after Bundy was executed, Jerry was able to retain the items as teaching tools for law enforcement seminars.

"You've got Ted Bundy's bag!" I said, my voice rising with excitement.

"Yes, I'm holding it right now." Feeling ashamed that I was feeling slightly exhilarated, I asked if he could meet me at the restaurant several minutes earlier than we'd planned so I could take a look for myself.

I quickly parked my car, jumped out and hurried over to Jim's truck just in time to see him coming around the rear holding the infamous brown leather bag. The satchel itself was in a clear plastic bag just large enough to cover it. With the care of a museum curator, Jim gently removed the plastic cover from Bundy's murder kit and laid the bag in the bed of his truck. With an anticipation that can only accompany a situation as surreal as this, we began removing, one piece at a time, the items once belonging to America's most infamous serial killer.

First, the woolen ski mask, and then a red-handled ice pick. Next, he retrieved a flashlight, then a long white piece of clothesline rope, then a smaller, orange-colored electrical cord. Bundy had also taken a white bed sheet and cut it into long strips for binding the hands and feet of his victims, and these were still bundled together with the FBI evidence tag. There were two right-handed gloves, a brown one made of nylon, the other a puffy ski-type, blue in color. Also within the bag were a woman's belt (no doubt from one of the murdered girls) and an opened box of Glad trash bags. Bundy always used plastic trash bags to dispose of his victims' clothes, and he always discarded them far from where he placed the bodies.

Needless to say, this made for interesting conversation that evening, as I had not expected something as peculiar as Theodore Bundy's murder kit to ever come my way, even if it was only for temporary viewing. But my adventure into the surreal was far from over. As Jim was allowed to keep the bag for the entire time the Thompsons were in town, he allowed me to transport the macabre cargo from his house to mine the following evening. It was around 9:30 p.m. when I called my wife from the car and told her what I was bringing into the house, quickly adding, "Clear everything off the dining room table, as I'll be taking plenty of photographs." As I closed my cell phone, I glanced at the bag lying next to me in the passenger seat and shook my head in amazement; after all, I thought, here I am driving through a neighborhood at night with the same bag Theodore Bundy carried as he went about similar neighborhoods years ago, trolling for victims. "Truly bizarre," I mumbled to myself as each passing street lamp bathed the infamous satchel in an eerie light.

Yet imagine my surprise, when two days later as we were saying our goodbyes to Detective Thompson and his wife, he offered to give Jim and me each one of the Glad bags from Bundy's car. Not believing my ears, I said yes, and immediately asked if he would be so kind as to write us a letter of authentication. Within minutes I was carrying home (to the consternation of my wife) one of Bundy's tools of the trade.

After this, I set about to write an article for *Snitch*, which was a weekly print newspaper devoted to issues of crime that was published in five or six states, and Kentucky ran editions in both Louisville and Lexington. Once finished, I titled that piece, *Three Days with Ted Bundy*, as everything happened over that period of days. I was thinking that, after being hyped up by interviewing Jerry and having that kit in my home (plus the Glad bag Jerry gave me from that kit), would all go away after the article was published. But that didn't happen. Instead, the drive to know more about Ted Bundy substantially increased, and driven by an inner knowing that writing a book about the killer was now a must, I began the long journey into the life and murders of Theodore Robert Bundy; a journey that occupied almost all of my time for the next 2 ½ years.

And even though I had friends, including my very well-intentioned friend, Jim Massie, telling me "Bundy's been done to death, why write a book about him?" Once my book was published and Jim read it, he changed his mind, saying he was glad I didn't listen to him!

So, despite the early opposition, it proved to be the right decision. Not only did I uncover new information on several of the murders, but I dug up a lot of new and general information on the case as well. I also wrote it from the perspective of the reader following Bundy every step of the way; which is a bit different from the other biographers of the killer. And without question, it was this book that launched my career as a true crime writer.

Meeting Jerry Thompson was great, and it's an experience I'll never forget. But more than anything else, it was having

Ted Bundy's murder kit in my home, as well as being given one of the Glad trash bags from the kit (Bundy would use these to discard the victim's clothes in dumpsters and other locations far away from where he placed the bodies), that spurred me onwards in my quest to learn everything I could about Bundy and the murders.

What a surreal experience it all was.

After the Thompsons returned home to Utah, Bundy's murder kit went back into storage in their home. And the following year, in August 2006, when I met Jerry Thompson at the Fashion Place Mall in Murray, Utah to interview him once again, I asked him what his intentions were concerning the murder kit once he no longer wants it; really meaning, once he passes on. He said that he would probably pass it on to his son who is also in law enforcement. I did mention he could always donate it to the Smithsonian Institution, or a police museum that might be interested in having it. And we spoke no more about it

And then, in 2019, Jerry died. And I guess it was a few months after this that, while corresponding with his wife, Jean, that I asked her what were her plans for the murder kit; quickly suggesting that she might want to contact the Smithsonian. I also mentioned that if the Smithsonian wasn't interested, I would be happy to call some folks I know in the FBI and I could have them contact her directly if the Smithsonian wasn't interested. She mentioned they were in contact with someone at the institution, and I said that's good and that's the last I heard about it.

Strangely, on October 31, 2019 (Halloween, how appropriate), TMZ heralded the following headline:

TED BUNDY
MURDER KIT SOLD TO ZAK BAGANS...
Ski Mask, Ice Pick, & More!!!

As it turns out, Zak Bagans became aware of the kit, and after contact was made with the Thompson family, the kit was sold for a substantial amount of money. No, it didn't end up at the Smithsonian, nor police or an FBI museum. However, Bagans has a crime museum in Las Vegas and he plans to display it there. So at least, for those traveling there, they'll be able to view Bundy's infamous tools of the trade of murder.

There is one caveat to the sale of the murder kit. When it came to Louisville, within the kit were evidence tins containing the pubic hair of a number of the victims (Melissa Smith, I believe Caryn Campbell, and there were others), plus the head hair of Carol DaRonch. These samples were obtained within Bundy's VW, for despite all the cleaning Bundy did, he missed a lot of evidence. Now, when I photographed the murder kit while it was in my home, you'd see these tins laying on the table. And just before the Thompsons returned to Utah, we met the couple at the Breckinridge Inn where they were staying, and Jim Massie took additional photos of the items, and one of these pics was the grouping of these tins, and this picture appears in *The Bundy Murders*. My point is this: while these tins were a part of the kit as evidence was fine; and photographing them was fine as well. But I'm hoping that was not a part of the sale and the tins removed, as I do not believe they should be either owned by anyone or displayed.

What Remains to Be Discovered About Bundy and His Murders?

Without question, there are other things to "turn up" in this case, especially in the form of testimonies from those valid contacts who may never have told their stories outside of what they told the police, and even here, they'll have stories and anecdotes that failed to hit the official record. I have had many verifiable Bundy contacts throughout the writing of six books on the case, and each one brought information to the printed page that was previously unknown, and some of it extraordinarily significant, as in the cases of Larry Anderson (*The Trail of Ted Bundy*); Louise Cannon (*The Bundy Secrets*); and Francine Bardole (*Ted Bundy's Murderous Mysteries)* just to name a few. So, there are still extremely important stories out there, and every one of them will add to the overall story of the Ted Bundy murders. So whenever writers have a chance to record their voices they're doing all of us a service.

And yet, there are some particular things I would like to know, such as, discovering the paternity of Ted Bundy. And I'm not just talking about who Bundy's biological father is, but *who he is not!* And of course, I'm referring to all the people who believe that Samuel Cowell, Bundy's grandfather, is actually Bundy's father. That would be great if we could finally put that one to rest, whatever the truth may be.

I would also like to see additional remains located that can be attributed to Bundy. I find it interesting that Bundy told investigators that those he buried have never been found. Where are they? Well, in the case of Taylor Mountain, that's the location where Bundy deposited the heads of Brenda Ball, Susan Rancourt, Lynda Ann Healy, and Kathy Parks. The rest of the remains are buried elsewhere; and that elsewhere may be Taylor Mountain. The reason I say that has to do with some additional human bones that were located on the mountain during the original March 1975 search (along with many animal bones too), but these remains were not DNA tested until 2005, at which time a member of each of the following families: the Rancourt family, the Ball family, and the Parks family came forward and gave samples to the authorities (the Healy family wanted nothing to do with it and gave no samples). And to no one's surprise, they were identified as being from

Ball, Parks and Rancourt. The only remaining unidentified remains are believed to be those of Lynda Ann Healy.

So, what happened? Most likely, Bundy severed the heads of the women, and perhaps kept each head a while. The bodies were no doubt buried on the mountain and partially rooted up by large animals leaving most of the remains still in the ground. One thing that seems certain is that had Bundy dumped the bodies on top of the ground and animals had fed upon them, there would have been far more skeletal remains in the area than were recovered. At Issaquah, a great deal of human remains were discovered, which is a natural occurrence when left on top of the ground as these victims were. What they never found were the skulls of Janice Ott and Georgann Hawkins. Bundy would tell Det. Bob Keppel that he buried Hawkins' head on a nearby hillside. But after this confession came forth in 1989, according to Keppel, the topography of the land had changed to such a degree they were unable to locate it.

After Bundy confessed to the abduction and murder of Debra Kent, also at the end of his life, and told the authorities the approximate location where he buried her and they did find a single patella (later DNA testing revealed it belonged to Debra Kent). They also found hundreds of animal bones, but no additional human remains. Why? Bundy said that he buried her in a two to three-foot grave, and piled rocks on top of it. And had she been totally unearthed by large predators, there would have been more of her to find. Recently, a friend of mine mentioned that perhaps a bird may have gotten ahold of the patella and flown off with it, which is absolutely possible. And if so, the mostly undisturbed grave of Debra Kent may be found if a more diligent search could be conducted. After all, if she's still out there, a proper burial would be in order for her.

Elizabeth Kendall and Her Daughter Molly

A couple of years before I decided to write a book about Ted Bundy, I was in a Half Price Books store here in Louisville, and I happened upon *The Phantom Prince*, By Elizabeth Kendall, sitting on the second shelf from the top. It had a price sticker of $5.98 on it (it wouldn't be many years before this same book would be selling for $100 or more) and because of my conversations with Jim Massie, I decided to buy it. I took the book home, skimmed it a bit, and placed it on my bookshelf to read at a later date. And then, when the opportunity arose for me to meet retired detective Jerry Thompson, and how that meeting led me to write about this infamous case, I was exceedingly happy I had purchased Liz Kendall's book. And I must say, the book contains a wealth of information about her time with Ted, and what those years were like for Liz and her daughter, Molly.

Of course, when I began to write *The Bundy Murders*, I decided to use the pseudonym Liz gave herself, and I purposely changed the name of Molly to Tina. I believe now, and have always believed, that folks who go through such things are better left alone. And so, after my book was published, I had a number of people ask me if I contacted her. I said no. When asked why not, I said I have her book and that's all the information I would need from her, adding, folks like this usually want to be left alone. Later, I learned from others who had tried to contact Liz, that she always referred them to her attorney, and this confirmed my suspicions. And frankly, a lot of people searching for her today (and this goes for members of the Bundy family as well), are not academics, researchers or even genuine writers. For some reason, and perhaps in ways they can't articulate themselves, they just want to connect. As a writer, I never connect with folks just to say "Hi!". If there is no real need to look for an individual, I won't do it. That's just my way of doing what I do.

A couple of years ago, a friend of mine who has been a researcher into the Bundy case for years, and has had major involvement with two Bundy documentaries, including the recent *Ted Bundy: Falling for a Killer,* has gotten to know Liz and speaks very highly of her, which is no surprise to me. From all I have heard, she's a very nice lady. And as I am always quick to remind people, she and her daughter Molly, are victims of Ted Bundy too; as is the Bundy family. So often, people are so quick to judge others for their actions, and it's always a mistake to do so.

My friend also told me (long before the general public had any details at all), that Liz was going to be in *Falling for a Killer*, and that she would be re-releasing her book. When I heard there would be a second edition of *Phantom,* I said, "Oh man" and laughed, because I knew the value of the 1st editions would drop precipitously. All joking aside, I was thrilled that a new generation would be reading Liz and Molly's story, many for the first time. I also learned that the book would have a slew of new pictures, which is so important to help tell the story. Of course, I pre-ordered it as soon as it was available on Amazon.

Now, I have to admit, that I'm rarely surprised about anything that happens in life. I guess it's the way I grew up, and I've seen a lot over the years. Plus, being immersed in the researching and writing of true crime for the last 25 years hasn't helped my cynicism either. Well, be that as it may, when I received the 2nd edition of The Phantom Prince, and read Molly's story of how Ted exposed himself to her as a little girl, I had two emotions: First, I actually felt "shock" that Bundy, deviant though he was, would not even control himself when it came to Molly. He was, in essence, a surrogate father to the child, and had to have recognized himself in that role, so why not make at least this relationship off limits to perversion? My second thought was this: My suspicions that (and this is something I've been saying for years) Bundy had more interest in very young girls than most people suspect, and that some of his unknown victims are likely this age. After all, we know that he killed Lynette Culver of Pocatello, Idaho and Kimberly Leach of Lake City, Florida, both of whom were 12 years old.

And we also know that when the stolen VW Bundy was driving in Florida was searched, they found a cheerleader magazine featuring young girls on teams. It is also a fact that in one of Bundy's third-person "confessions" as to what serial killers do, he referred to one killer (in my opinion, himself), and said that person killed as many as half a dozen young girls. And of course, we will never know all there is to know about his murders, but whenever additional and valid information is released, as in Molly's story, it's a good thing and one that will aid us in our understanding of Ted Bundy.

Lastly, it was good seeing Liz and Molly on the documentary, and it appears they are doing well. And in the end, that's all that matters.

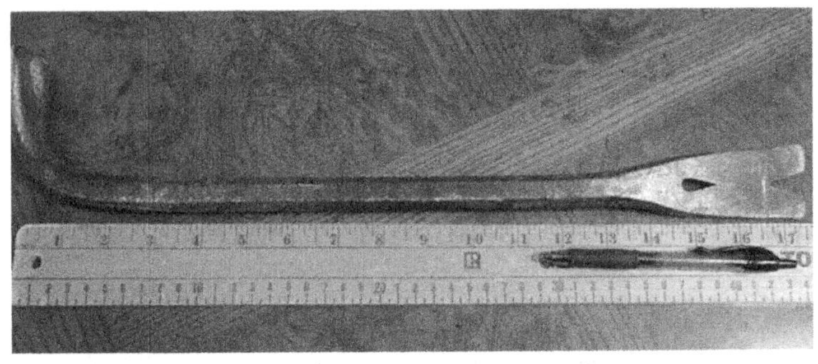

Slightly under 18 inches, this is the type of crowbar Bundy carried. Being the shortest crowbar manufactured, it gave Bundy easy maneuverability to strike his victims in the cramped space of his VW, or to hide it beneath the rear of his car.

Ted Bundy's Crowbar of Choice

As a Utah police report reveals, Bundy carried as part of his tools of murder, a 6577 Sears model crowbar. In reality, it wasn't important it was from Sears, what mattered to Bundy was the size of the crowbar, only 18 inches (I've also seen some old advertisements stating it was 17 inches). The reason why Bundy wanted the shorter version crowbar was because it gave him the ability to easily wield it in his car if he had a passenger in the passenger seat. Placing this rather small but heavy iron tool right behind the seat would give him an edge he wouldn't have with the longer version. It was also easier to conceal behind the right rear of his car; right behind the passenger side of the vehicle. Bundy would use this type of concealment to capture Georgann Hawkins, Susan Rancourt, and Julie Cunningham, just to name a few. He believed it would be the perfect tool for attacking his victims, and he was right.

A postscript to the issue of Ted's short crowbar (or one exactly like it) became a part of my story a few years ago as my wife and I were driving home from a steakhouse on a weeknight here in Louisville. As I turned left onto

Taylorsville Road from Cannons Lane, I spotted a short crowbar just lying in the middle of the road. As I passed it, I thought to myself it looked exactly like an old Sears model 6577 crowbar, or one identical to it. As I mentioned it to my wife, she said I should go back and get it. I said "Nah" but almost immediately thought, yes, maybe I will as I'm certain I'll never again drive by an "antique" crowbar just lying in the road. And it's that crowbar–along with a yardstick showing its length–that I've used for this book so that you'll see why Bundy preferred it.

CHAPTER FOUR

JAMES MASSIE

I first met James Massie (Jim to his friends) in 1995 and we hit it off immediately. He was a Probation and Parole Officer for the state of Kentucky, and I was a minister and a fledgling writer with an interest in history and true crime. Both our fathers had been in WW2 (everybody I grew up with, it seems, had a dad serve in WW2), and we were both voracious readers of war, all things true crime, and a splash of other subjects thrown in. Jim also had a great sense of humor and we had many a laugh whenever we got together. Although we talked on the phone a great deal, and I often visited his home, every Wednesday night for years we met for coffee at a local bookstore. And of course, as many of you know, Jim was the unintentional catalyst causing me to write about Ted Bundy. But more about that in a minute.

In the early 1980s, Jim traveled to Utah to do research on the murders in that state, and in the process, met and became friends with Det. Jerry Thompson of the Salt Lake County Sherriff's Office, and Dr. Al Carlisle, the psychologist who examined Ted Bundy for the state of Utah. Jim also got to know Dean and Belva Kent, and became very good friends with Jim Aime, the father of murder victim, Laura Ann Aime (because Jim Aime knew of Jim's interest in WW2, he gave him a Japanese Army bayonet a family member had brought home from the war). And so, when Jerry Thompson told Jim in March of 2005 that he and his wife were coming to Louisville in May, he invited me to have dinner with them; something I immediately agreed to as I considered it a once in a lifetime chance to meet one of the detectives from the Bundy case.

It wasn't like I knew a lot about Bundy, mind you, at least not in depth. I knew he had been executed in 1989 for the murder of a young girl in Florida, and that he was suspected of many murders in the Pacific Northwest and beyond. I also remember Bundy first came on my radar after his escape in Colorado (and I remember thinking after his final escape, "I hope he doesn't come through Louisville"—because of the women here, and I found out later that's exactly what Bundy did!), and that when he told Doctor James Dobson at the end that pornography was to blame for the murders, he was lying. But as to real knowledge of the case? No, not even close.

And so, after meeting Jerry and his wife, and viewing Bundy's murder kit that Thompson brought with him, I decided to write a book about Ted Bundy. And now that I was "in" with Jerry, I asked Jim if he could ask Al Carlisle if I could interview him too. And after Al said yes, I telephoned him and in no time, we became friends, and even beyond my writing *The Bundy Murders*, we kept up with each other over the years. And the same was true with Jerry. And having made (through Jim) a great start to my investigation into the Utah murders, he also mentioned he knew Mike Fisher, the Colorado investigator, and Don Patchen, the lead detective in the Chi Omega murders in Florida, and that when I tracked them down, I should mention we're friends, which I did.

So, Jim Massie played an instrumental role in helping me in the early stages of my research, and he put me in touch with some very important people closely connected to the case. There were, of course, many more people to find, and over the next year or so I found them all. But Jim's initial efforts really made a difference, and for that I am eternally grateful.

I should mention too, that long before I met Jim, he'd been working with Ron Holmes, a well-known criminologist, who was also working with (or soon would be) Ted Bundy. In fact, they were supposed to visit Bundy in his Florida prison to do a filmed interview with the killer. That fell through after the two men had had a falling out, and we'll get more into that in a few minutes. Still, Holmes had already been to Florida once to interview the killer, and the two men exchanged many letters (Jim had copies of these letters, and I was able to read them a few years before writing my book). What follows is from the Acknowledgments section of Holmes' book, *Serial Murder*, co-authored with James De Burger and published in 1988:

...and Jim Massie, Parole Officer for the state of Kentucky, whose interests in serial murder aided us in getting valuable information on Bundy.

Ron Holmes continued to acknowledge Jim in his other published works in the future, which I know Jim appreciated, as he had made at least two trips to Utah in the early 1980s to investigate and gather information there. What follows is from my second book on the Bundy case, *The Trail of Ted Bundy: Digging Up the Untold Stories*:

The final piece of the Laura Aime connection has to do with my late friend James Massie, who originally introduced me to Jerry Thompson, for without Jim's introduction, The Bundy Murders would never have been written, and you wouldn't be reading these words either. Anyway, in the early 1980s, Jim traveled to Utah to conduct research and meet some of the families of the victims and others involved in the case. I believe it was at this time that he was introduced to Detective Jerry Thompson and Dr. Al Carlisle.

One of the families Jim grew close to was the Aime family and especially to Jim Aime. The two men got along well, and as can be expected, his grief was just under the surface of his personality. One day as the two men were driving past the spot where Laura had been found, Jim

Aime blurted out, "My little baby was up there all by herself and there was nothing I could do to help her." Jim Massie also believed that Jim Aime passed away well before his time due to his daughter's murder and the distress that he suffered because of her death.

I must also say that it was my intention to transcribe the taped interview I did with Jim from 2007, but I have not been able to locate it. I was able to transcribe the taped interviews of Don Patchen, Jerry Thompson, and Ronald M. Holmes. So, if you're reading these words, it means I never located the tape between "now" and when this book went to press. Even so, this is a nice tribute to my friend in what will be my final book on the Bundy case.

Now, before we begin the transcripts, I wanted to pass along two versions of how Bundy and Holmes had a falling out. In Holmes' version (which you'll read in his transcript), it has to do with Bundy asking him to purchase a desktop computer for Carole Boone, as Carole was going back to school. Of course, Bundy always was a user and whatever he thought he could get out of people, he would shamelessly try. Well, upon hearing this, Holmes told Bundy no, he wouldn't do that; that if he bought a computer it was going to be for one of his children. And that's the "official" version given by Ron Holmes.

Jim Massie, however, gave another version. According to Jim, Holmes had written an article for a governmental publication and had sent a copy to Bundy, which immediately made the killer mad. And in the transcript, there is a mention of such a magazine article and it could be what Jim was referring to in our conversation. Jim, who would often put a funny spin to things said, "So, in the end, Holmes peed in his Wheaties!" "What?!" I blurted out. "Holmes peed in his Wheaties," Jim said, "and he blew the deal with Bundy and it was cancelled." I think Jim was looking forward to seeing Bundy up close and personal after all the investigations he had done on his Utah murders.

What's the actual truth to why a good (on the surface) relationship between the two men abruptly came to a screeching halt? Well, Bob Keppel once told me that he believed Holmes was Bundy's "golden boy" and had every intention of confessing all his crimes to him, and I believe Keppel was right. So, to have such an abrupt dissolution means something quickly came to a head, and perhaps both stories may have played a part and came about at the same time.

Jim Massie passed away at the age of 66 in 2011. Ronald M. Holmes died at the age of 81 in 2020.

CHAPTER FIVE

THE TAPED INTERVIEWS

During my research for *The Bundy Murders: A Comprehensive History,* I conducted many interviews for the book, and the gathering of information happened in several ways. In some cases, I conducted phone interviews and took detailed notes. Sometimes these conversations provided additional communications, including detailed emails from the interviewees who took the time to write out their experiences in even greater depth and provided their testimony by way of a written record, and it was generous of them to do so. And at other times, circumstances allowed me to sit down with them and record their thoughts and remembrances of this most infamous case. As such, I will be presenting three such interviews that are enlightening to the Bundy case.

Two of these will be with detectives who played major roles in the investigation: the late lead Utah investigator, Det. Jerry Thompson of the Salt Lake County Sheriff's Office, and Det. Don Patchen, lead investigator for the Chi Omega murders for the Tallahassee Police Department. The Thompson interview was conducted in August 2006 at the Fashion Place Mall in Murray, Utah, and the Patchen interview was recorded in June 2008 at his home in Tallahassee, Florida.

Ron Holmes, the late Louisville criminologist, who had worked with Ted Bundy, and who was, according to Washington State detective for the Bundy case, Bob

Keppel, "Bundy's golden boy" whom Bundy would have confessed all his murders to had they not had a falling out, is here as well.

I must say, that after 14 years, there's a great deal of information that had slipped out of my memory. And so, as I listened to these tapes for the first time in many years, I was surprised to see how much really important information was there—all of which gives great insight into the minds of these two detectives as they went toe to toe with a Ted Bundy they knew was guilty and they just had to prove it. You'll also learn of Ronald Holmes' dealing with the killer, and he goes in-depth concerning what makes serial murderers "tick", as well as how killing without motive makes solving such murders far more difficult.

Moreover, when I taped these interviews, I never had any intentions of transcribing and publishing them in any format, including books. And, as with any research one gathers when writing a book, you pick the material you want to use, that which best expresses the heart of what you want to address, and the rest may lie dormant for another time. But when I made the decision to publish these tapes in their entirety, it sounded like a very good idea. But once I started re-listening to them, I knew I had something very special on my hands. It was almost like these tapes were created for such a moment where I could use them in their entirety, which is something I couldn't do when I was writing *The Bundy Murders: A Comprehensive History*.

A note about how I created these transcripts from the taped interviews: First, I identify myself with my initials, KS. The interviewee with his initials. When a statement by myself or the interviewee isn't as clear as it needs to be, I will amplify the answer (or my question) with further information, and this will appear in brackets. Finally, there are some quotes I use in *The Bundy Murders* from all of these individuals that are not on these tapes, where I received them either through phone conversations or emails, and in these cases, my publisher required that I obtain signed and dated release statements from them, thereby assuring that I have quoted them accurately. At the same time, I asked for (and received) permission to publish their statements and communications ‘as is’. And when you’re publishing such statements, it’s always good to be crossing one’s “T’s” and dotting one’s “I’s”. For the taped interviews, however, one doesn’t need special permission, for special permission is assumed when an interviewee agrees to a taped interview.

What follows are the transcripts I made directly from the tapes, beginning with Detective Jerry Thompson…

Jerry and Jean Thompson in Louisville, Ky, where they met the author in May 2005

JERRY THOMPSON

Jerry Thompson
August 15, 2006
The Fashion Place Mall

KS: On October 2, 1974, Nancy Wilcox disappeared from Holiday (Utah)…that was under the Sheriff's jurisdiction, right?

JT: Yes.

KS: Were you assigned to the case?

JT: Well, you've got to understand, I didn't work all these cases, I was a coordinator (*re the Bundy cases, once they saw a pattern and knew they had a single killer out there*), and as we got everything we could put it together. Her case was never handled by us but was with the Juvenile Division up until the very end (*when her case was finally linked to Bundy)*. So, I can't tell you much about it.

KS: Was this case considered routine? There was nothing to make you think it was committed by Bundy?

JT: I never did have anything that could tie it to him.

KS: When Melissa Smith disappeared, on October 18, and I know you knew her father…

JT: Yeah, chief of police of Midvale…

KS: Yes, my God, can you imagine that, and he turned the investigation over to you, I guess?

JT: That's true, and it was a case where we had no evidence to link him to it.

KS: Yeah, he left no evidence at the scene?

JT: No evidence.

KS: Is he still around?

JT: No.

KS: How did Chief Smith handle her death?

JT: He had a rough time; a lot of problems. He just had a very tough time.

KS: And you knew her (Melissa)?

JT: I didn't know her, no, I knew of her.

KS: Okay, okay.

KS: When Laura Aime disappeared, even though that was not in your jurisdiction…

JT: Utah County.

KS: Yeah, and I know as things developed there, later on, after Bundy's arrest, he (*Sheriff Mack Holley*) didn't want any part of that (*Bundy being the one responsible*) …

JT: Yeah, they said "we'll handle it, we don't think it's connected with anything you guys got." And we had a difficult time with that. Later, an investigator for Utah County worked with our investigators and got into the idea it was Bundy, but early on…

KS: When Laura went missing, and you first heard about it, was there anything in your mind that got the wheels turning that Wilcox, Smith and Aime were connected?

JT: No, no, I never did, I never did…Wilcox was considered a runaway and Aime was a homicide.

KS: What was your first meeting with Ted Bundy like, face-to-face?

JT: Ah, he was an individual that, ah, it's hard to describe it; I'll try to describe it. He was jovial, laughing and joking, he was so nice, so cooperative he was, ah, putting me on the defensive immediately because he was so cooperative.

KS: At what point in your dealing with him, apparently he liked to taunt the police, and I know he said to you "you found a straw and maybe if you keep looking you'll find another straw and maybe you can put a broom together…"

JT: Yeah, yeah, I can't remember the exact…

KS: He was taunting you…

JT: Yes, he did. I mean, how many suspects do you get that follows a policeman? (*Bundy followed Thompson when he visited the University of Utah Law School to pick up copies of his grades and interview his teachers*)

KS: Yes.

JT: He considered himself far superior to anyone else; smarter than anyone else, he (*believed*) he could outwit everybody.

KS: Were you surprised he made such a statement; a taunt?

JT: Yeah, it was kinda surprising he would make a comment like that. That he would follow me around the University of Utah and around different places. On surveillance, he picked out some of the guys on surveillance and he would wave…yeah, I knew he was playing games.

KS: You know, when Forbes (*Det. Ben Forbes*) was dealing with him one time, Bundy thought he wanted to talk about the stuff he had with him in his VW, the "burglary tools", but Forbes came out and said, "My game is homicide!"

JT: I didn't know, because I wasn't in on that interview, but I know about it because Ben Forbes was my partner…and I know it got Bundy's attention.

KS: Yeah, I guess it did. You know, in the trial, which was recorded (*minimally*) in Michaud's book, where Yocom mentions Forbes as Forbes had told him all about it, and I do think it made an impression on Bundy. Another thing, did you get to sit in on the trial of Carol DaRonch?

JT: I was locked, I was excluded, they wouldn't let me in there. They didn't want me there. The only time I was there I was asked to be in there when they were going to read the verdict.

KS: Bundy made a statement to Yocom, something along the lines like why would he have used a crowbar in the car, as a way, I suppose, of derailing Carol DaRonch's statement that he attacked her (*with it*).

JT: Oh yeah, he had an answer for everything.

KS: When you read the transcript, it looks like Bundy is saying why would he have done something like this, like he was playing with the authorities.

JT: He thought he was better than anyone else, no doubt about it, if you had seen him in court, he would try to turn things around on you.

KS: What did you begin to think about Bundy, as you got to know him, what were your feelings about him, did you get to where you saw him as a pure sociopath?

JT: Yeah, I knew, let's put it this way, the further I got into it, the more and deeper I got into it, I was trying to figure what kind of man he was, and I don't think I missed it too far, especially around girls—they thought the world of him like he walked on water. Well, he was a leech, every girl he went with he always sponged off of them. If he wanted a beer, they would pay for it. They all recognized him as a leech and that he used them. He took advantage of them to get whatever he wanted…a lot of these women would come to see him after a time for what he really was.

KS: Did you ever see him become angry with you or any of the other detectives?

JT: Not here but (*inaudible*) I'm very, very upset with Colorado and what happened over there. They had to remove him from the courtroom; I wasn't there at the moment, but when the officers brought him out of the courtroom, he was (*inaudible*) he was like a maniac (*in his expression*).

KS: Well, there is something diabolical about Ted Bundy. I know you've mentioned his eyes in other conversations we've had about how his eyes would become really different, and I know Michaud said some things about his eyes, as did Larsen (*Richard Larsen*).

JT: Yes, I've seen it quite a bit.

KS: Michaud said (*I'm quoting from his book, The Only Living Witness*) "There was a cold poisonous luster in Bundy's unguarded gaze. I had heard about it before I met him, but I was unprepared for its effect. When his entity retreated, a softer blue came into Ted's eyes. His irises clear and his pupils constricted. His expression went from sinister to mild in a moment."

JT: His eyes, there was something about his eyes that bothered me…the pupils in his eyes, cold black, cold black; there was a difference when I talked to him, it was like looking at a monster— his demeanor changed several times when you were hitting him with different things—cause and effect.

KS: I remember reading something (*Author's note: at this time when I was interviewing Jerry, I was unaware that the following event happened as Bundy was conferring with his own people— attorneys, etc—I was assuming it happened under the grilling of the detectives, but that was incorrect. The rest of the information as to what happened to Bundy is accurate.*) about who was grilling him in Florida, when the body of the little Leach girl was found (*Kim Leach, 12, was his last victim and was abducted and murdered by him on February 9, 1978.*), and not just his demeaner changed, (*but*) muscle tone and smell; it's like he was transforming and some of these guys found it troubling.

JT: When they brought that up, that really troubled me, really, really troubled me (*that she was so young*) and at that time, she was the only one (*of that age*) we knew about.

KS: You know, you must have been really shocked when Colorado let him go, not once, but twice.

JT: Yes, I was not a happy individual. And Fisher (*Mike Fisher, the Colorado investigator*) was fit to be tied. I warned them in Colorado, "You're not watching this guy, you're leaving him alone. He's going down to the Coke machine", they'd say, "Oh, Jerry, this guy's not going to do anything, we could make him a trustee," (*Jerry adding what they said:*) "he's not going to do this, he's not going to do that." I said, "You know, this guy is accused of murder." They said, "He doesn't give us any trouble" (*Jerry responded*) I told them, I told them at one of the hearings we had over there, "You know what, ah, I don't usually carry my side arm when I'm here, but I don't trust you guys (*to watch him*) you totally turn your back" (*meaning, Bundy might be able to escape, and Thompson wanted to be armed to stop him with force if necessary.)*

KS: Did you have any conversations with these guys after his escapes?

JT: Oh, several times, I told them somebody's going to get killed, so I rubbed it in, and they didn't appreciate me after that. In fact, I remember, I told some of the families (*these were families of the Florida victims*), some families got a hold of me and asked if they could get attorneys and file suits, and I said you'll have to talk to the attorneys, that's out of my ballpark. But they asked several times about it. When Bundy got out of jail (*escaped the second time*) that was a joke too, they'd been warned by numerous inmates that Bundy was up crawling around in the attic; they could hear him crawling around above them at night.

KS: When Bundy was unable to abduct Carol DaRonch, he went up to Bountiful to Viewmont High School, I was there today and I photographed the inside of the hallway and the auditorium where there were some 1500 people waiting to see the play. Can you imagine the audacity of Bundy, and in view of that many people and rip this girl off?

JT: Well, he was very confident, he had a lot of experience by then, he had an ego thing about women, and it wasn't wrong—that he could attract women. (*At this point in the interview, it is very loud in the food court where we're sitting, and there are numerous gaps where our conversation is inaudible. But as we started to discuss the abduction of Debra Kent, it starts to quiet down to the point the words are clearly heard on the tape.)*

KS: Jerry, I understand Bundy would call you while he was in jail, is that correct?

JT: Oh, he would call me all the time, just all the time, and I'd talk to him. Because he was helping to represent himself, the jail allowed it. He would ask me something and I would say, "Where's Debbie" and he would laugh and say "Who's Debbie!" He didn't like me asking about Debra Kent, but I did it whenever he called. I said, "You claim you got a conscience, tell me about Debbie. How would you like your parents to not know where you were at?" Well, he'd say, "That was a way's back", and I said "No, you know more about that stuff than anybody." (*Here's another example Jerry gave me over the phone one day, and I used it in The Bundy Murders: "Bundy declared he couldn't be involved in the things he was suspected of, as he, too, had a conscience. "If you have a conscience," Thompson fired back, "tell me about Debbie!" (referring to Debra Kent). "Ah, Debbie," Bundy shouted through the receiver, and started laughing. "I don't know anything about Debbie. You will have to ask someone else about that.")*

KS: When was the last time you saw him?

JT. That would be in court in Colorado.

KS: Finally, I know the story about you and the other detectives going up to his apartment to serve him a summons to appear in a line up. And I know Bundy became afraid that you might have been there to arrest him for one of the murders, because you all saw his heart beating in his chest (*Bundy was shirtless, having just gotten out of the shower*). What did you think of that?

JT: I thought he was going to die of heart failure. (*Laughter*)

RONALD M. HOLMES

Ronald M. Holmes
January 7, 2007
Office of the Coroner
Louisville, Ky

KS: Now, Ron, you first interviewed Ted (*in person*), in August of 1987?

RH: Yes

KS: Had you corresponded prior to that time?

RH: We wrote back and forth for at least six months, and ah, my first letter was introducing myself, you know, could I talk to him? I already had an article in Federal Probation on serial murder, and he wanted that article, which I copied, and he wanted my resume; he just wanted to make sure who I was, and ah, and so we corresponded, like I say, six months before I went down.

KS: Before your contact with Ted, had you read Michaud and Aynesworth's *The Only Living Witness*?

RH: Yes.

KS: Did you think you were dealing with the same kind of person? Do you think Bundy had changed any in his personality by being incarcerated? Did you notice any kinds of changes with him from how he was with Michaud?

RH: Ah, he used the same techniques with me as he did with them. He talked about "I didn't do anything but if I had", or "That person we're talking about". He never admitted that he did anything on a personal level, "This person we're talking about".

KS: What was your first impression of him, I mean, when you first met him, you probably had an impression of him prior to your face-to-face meeting with him of course, but what was your actual impression of him seeing him and observing him for the first time?

RH: I liked Ted, ah, he was very charming, articulate, verbal, he said all the things I wanted to hear. After four hours together, three and a half together, he had to go to lunch, so we broke up and I went to the cafeteria, snack bar they had. And ah, I was pleased with the way things were going. I went back and we had another three hours or so. I left the prison, I'm not sure, about 4:00 p.m. and drove back to Jacksonville where I was staying. Halfway back, I guess, I pulled my car off to the side of the road (*then Holmes corrects himself*); St. Augustine, not Jacksonville, I pulled my car off the side of the road, and I was firmly convinced this guy was innocent. He had me wrapped around his finger. And even though I'd seen reports and pictures from Jerry Thompson from Salt Lake City, and some stuff from Don Patchen in Tallahassee, read some reports, but I was mad at myself (*inaudible*) because the guy was so good. You know, I thought to myself, and still think, he'd be a good neighbor, take out the garbage for you, check the mail, but that 1% took over the 99%, and he became a totally different person.

KS: What do you think it was that caused him to become what he was, because, I'm sure, as a little boy, he didn't aspire to become what he was; however, what were the factors that created Ted Bundy?

RH: Ah, I had an article published in one of the journals called "Fractured Identity Syndrome", something that goes on very early in a person's life that causes a fracture, so to speak, in the personality, ah, it can be discovering you're illegitimate, you know, discovering your mother is actually your sister or your sister is actually your mother. But we all go through that, not that scenario but hurt in our young years; you have, I have, but I think it is that unique combination of timing and event that points some people toward a disposition that is opposite (*inaudible*), just because you're a sociopath doesn't mean you're the same kind of sociopath—some politicians have sociopathic qualities—I think Bundy, for whatever reason, I've heard, I read…that Ted was very upset because his grandfather was brutal, I asked him about his parents and grandparents. He never talked about his grandfather being cruel to animals…I don't know, and if anybody tells you they know, they're lying. It's that strange combination between timing and event, and it manifests itself very early, 12 – 13, during puberty, and it seems like (*inaudible*.)

KS: Did he say anything about his friends?

RH: Not that I know of, not that I know of. I think people liked Ted, coupled with his intelligence, he developed, as we all do, what somebody called that "on-stage behavior" and that "back-stage behavior". Your on-stage behavior is what you want people to see, and you know, your back-stage behavior is who you actually are. And most like to present a good image, and I think Ted was very interested in portraying, you know, in control, I'm a law student, on my way to law school one morning, and I get arrested. Ah, for whatever reason, I think he was able to do it and I think if we look for one cause, I don't think it's one cause, you know, a lot of kids learn they're illegitimate and it creates pain, but it doesn't cause them to be Ted Bundy.

KS: And since we cannot know for sure, it's pure speculation to wonder, do you feel he could have been helped to the degree he wouldn't have committed those acts?

RH: Well, he was good at hiding things that, you know, he was kind of ah, shy, and the reason I think he was shy was different from the reasons that I was shy or you were shy; in high school, 14 or 15 years-old. In high school he knew what he was about, these very violent fantasies—at 15 he killed his first victim, when I was 15, I was thinking how to take a girl out; yeah, that's where I was. (*Holmes is referring here to the murder of eight-year-old, Ann Marie Burr in Tacoma in 1961. If Bundy did commit this murder, he would have been 14. There are reasons to believe Bundy killed her, as he said cryptic things about it while alluding to her murder with Ron Holmes, and I have more detail about this unsolved murder in my book, The Bundy Murders.*) Lastly, it is of interest to note that in 2011, DNA taken from a vial of Bundy's blood was tested against the scant material they had from the Burr evidence that might rule Bundy either in or out of the case. However, because there was little to test, nothing came back connecting Ted Bundy to Ann Marie Burr's disappearance. That said, he is still considered a suspect by some, because of his statements to Ron Holmes.)

KS: Now, are you speaking of the Burr girl?

RH: Yeah.

KS: You know, I spoke with Bob Keppel about that and he said his killing started way before '74. Did he ever admit to that as far as we know?

RH: He said that this guy's victim was two years after his involvement with pornography, (*inaudible*) his involvement with pornography was when he was 13 (*Bundy would have been 12*). He said he would go back in the alleyways and would look in people's garbage cans and get *True Detective*

Story magazines, and he got to know what guy would read *True Detective* Story magazines, so he would check out the garbage cans. He said after two years he had to act it out.

KS: Someone mentioned, I can't remember now, he did not admit, actually, come out and admit because of embarrassment—his mother—do you believe that had something to do with it?

RH: Yeah, I talked to a guy in prison in Oregon who was in for the murder of two 12-year-old girls and he freely talks about the adults he has killed, 18, 19 years-old, he'll talk about that, but, but the kids put him in a whole different category (*inaudible*).

KS: Ah, Susan Rancourt knew Storwick (*Terry Storwick, Bundy's childhood friend*) and they even went jogging together. It makes you wonder with Ted, was it random with Rancourt?

RH: I don't think Ted did anything completely at random. That girl, the high school girl, I can't remember her name, Golden, Colorado, ah, there's so many names…

KS: So many names…

RH: Even with her you wonder how random it was, like the next person who comes through the door I'm gonna kill. But Ted was too organized for that. I'm sure he stalked her for some time. But driving up on a random hitchhiker, I don't think Ted would do that.

Author's note: It is important here to give some perspective about the things based on the totality of what we know about Ted Bundy from both the record and what he said in his final confessions. For example, while Ted was an exceedingly good planner of murder in Washington State, and to a far lesser extent in Utah and the other states in which he hunted; and while it is likely Ted either knew (but was not friends with) Lynda Ann Healy or perhaps knew of her (and it's a fact he knew there were coeds living in the house he'd ultimately attack), as to who he was abducting, it was random or, shall we say, just a matter of chance. But it is also clear, in fact very clear, that when Bundy was out hunting women, those falling victim to him were often falling by chance, simply being at the wrong place at the wrong time and succumbing to his wiles and trickery. Examples would be: Caryn Campbell (Wildwood Inn, where Bundy saw advantages and hatched a bit of a plan, but still depended on the randomness of the situation as to who would follow him to their deaths); Debra Kent (Viewmont High); Denise Oliverson (Grand Junction bicycle ride); Donna Manson (a quick walk to a concert on a college campus). And, as to Holmes' assertion that Bundy, because he couldn't "plan it", would not have picked up and murdered hitchhikers, misses the mark by at least two murders: the hitchhiker Bundy killed on his way to attending law school in the early morning hours of September 3, 1974 (Bundy left on the 2nd), and the hitchhiker he picked up in Tumwater, WA and murdered in 1973.

KS: Did Ted do with you what he had done with Stephen Michaud: "This person who killed. He might have done this, or he might have done that?

RH: Yes, with Georgann Hawkins he said "probably this guy…" and I told him, "If I'm called to testify I don't have that confidentiality thing; I'd have to tell them what you said", and you know, I told him right up front I don't have privilege, I wish I did. And I guess that's one reason he liked that third-person thing.

KS: Did you speak at all about Chi Omega?

RH: He wouldn't talk about that. He did talk about how the guy could have gotten in; he talked about the dance at

Sherrod's (*next door to Chi Omega*) but ah, he wouldn't talk specifically about the case (*inaudible*) because at the Chi Omega house on the first floor at the time they never locked the front door because the girls came in late at night. So when I was down there I went over to Chi Omega and they showed me around. They did start locking the doors after that. They also had a directory on the first floor—Lisa Levy, Margaret Bowman—and if you knew who you were looking for you could find them.

KS: Did Ted ever speak of, in detail, about any other victims, besides Georgann Hawkins; did he ever go into, for instance, the girls at Lake Sammamish?

RH: The only thing he talked about is that "There are some you don't know about…there's one in Vermont." I said how many people are we talking about, you told Don Patchen 33, 34, and you said to add one digit to that. Now is that a 134, or is that at 34, 35, or is that 351? Well, he said, "It's more than 350." Now, I don't know how accurate that is. I asked him, how many states are we talking about, and he said, "How many do you think." Washington, Oregon, I went through nine states, Vermont, and when I went through the nine states, he said "You missed one" So he confessed to that 10th one several days before he was executed. (*that would be Idaho, where he killed a hitchhiker and Lynette Culver*)

KS: Bundy was quite a killing machine. Does it surprise you how long he got away with murder?

RH: Well, he killed by himself, that's number one. He didn't tell anybody, and he killed strangers. He was geographically transient (*inaudible*).

KS: What do you think about these people who throw out these numbers of those who are committing serial murders operating at any one time? And how many do you think there might be?

RH: If you can find a serial killer, someone who kills three or more in a 30-day period, I think it's likely there are at least two per state. However, with large states, California, New Jersey, etc., there's a lot more there.

KS: Can you tell me about some of the changes which occurred in Bundy during his time of murder; and I mean pertaining to the actual murders, and not how he changed over time in general?

RH: When you get to the point, when you've been fantasizing what you're going to do, when you're a sadist; when you're preparing, the pain (*you're going to inflict during the attack*) is not as important as the anticipation of the pain (*inaudible*), it's not stress because he knows he's not going to be caught, it's the anticipation of the pain, and you know you're going to do the most pleasurable experience. You know, when I teach the murder classes, I tell the kids (*college students*) picture the most pleasurable thing, how excited you are and how ready you are, it's almost a letdown when you do it. If I had a fantasy of killing so and so, blond hair, blue eyes, shapely and young, if I see her and I fantasize what I'm going to do to her, and do these things, it never measures up. So, what I have to do is do it again. And next time (*the killer says to himself*) it's going to be better.

KS: Now, let me ask you about Chi Omega. It was so different; it was like a rampage.

RH: Yeah it was, because he hadn't killed in 2 ½ years. He's been locked up, he escapes, so the character of the crime scene at Chi Omega was like a disorganized crime scene. But what he did later, three weeks later (*Kimberly Leach murder*) he went back to the way he was killing out west, because he had had a "meal". Say, for example, you ran a marathon, say five miles and you go back to your home, and you're really thirsty, and you drink and drink. And an hour later, you might go over and get a drink again. So what Ted did at Chi Omega, if I had pulled the Chi Omega case, it didn't look like him. But the Kimberly Leach case did.

KS: What's your feeling…do you believe Bundy, either free or incarcerated, ever wanted—was there ever a time you believe he wanted help?

RH: No.

KS: I asked Al Carlisle that, and he said no too. (*laughter*)

RH: Al's a good guy!

KS: Al said there were times when Bundy wanted to speak with people, but to seek help, no.

RH: Yes.

KS: During your meeting with Bundy, your face-to-face meeting, was there a time when you felt Ted was being less than honest with you?

RH: Other than him saying no, I didn't do it, nah, I thought he was being as honest as he could be.

KS: After you left Florida, you continued to correspond with Ted. Did he elaborate on anything of significance to you?

RH: No, what happened was we corresponded back and forth six or seven times, and his wife apparently, ah, wanted to get into, or was accepted into the graduate program at the University of Florida, Carole Boone, and he wanted me to buy her a computer. I told him if I was going to buy anyone a computer, it would be one of my kids. And that was the end; Ted was a user. He got me in there, and it was Ron this and Ron that, he said "You truly have an understanding of the mind and mentality of a serial killer," and bam! He wanted me to do something for him. He also told me he wanted me to send mail to him and on the outside of the envelope, it should say "legal mail", so they wouldn't open it and I said no, I wouldn't do that. I wasn't going to hang myself out there. So that was pretty much the end after that.

KS: How do you think Bundy differed from the other serial killers you've interviewed?

RH: Well, he's the most educated and ah, I think he knew how to verbalize in situations for his own good. He's the epitome of just the opposite of what we think a serial killer is; a law student couldn't do this, you know. And yet, he never completed a semester, never completed his exams.

KS: Do people still call you and ask you about Bundy"

RH: Once in a while, it (*seeing him*) was a good career move. (*laughter*)

A final note on my interview with Ron Holmes. When I was interviewing him, his office phone rang twice. The first call was his wife, but the second call was from Stephen Michaud, the author of *The Only Living Witness* and *Confessions of a Killer*. Each time the phone rang, I naturally turned off the recorder. However, had I known it was from Michaud, I would have kept the tape running.

DON PATCHEN

Don Patchen
Tallahassee, Florida
June 26, 2008

KS: I'm with Don Patchen, the retired homicide detective with the Tallahassee Police Department. Today is the 26th of June 2008. Don, what was your feeling when you first got a call from the Pensacola Police Department about this Misner fellow who had some 21 stolen credit cards and some material from FSU coeds? Did you think, because you were working the Chi Omega case, did you think there could be a connection; did that come into your mind?

DP: (*Laugh*) I was dead asleep and the dispatcher woke me up, about a call from Pensacola, an officer had stopped a person in a VW trolling...he had his lights off driving around in the dark, and ah, ah, and of course it was in a VW. And of course, this area, these murders were very much in the news. I called, and they told me who to call, it was Norman Chapman. I called him and ah, he ah, told me that an officer, David Lee, had stopped an individual, a VW, and had a lot of credit cards and things in the VW that were stolen out of Tallahassee. Well, that real quick, as far as my mind...in today's line, a person of interest (*laughs*) a suspect, the same term—anyway, I got up and I called Steve Bodiford who had been working the case with me for the Leon County Sheriff's Office, and ah, we threw together some clothes, we didn't even think we'd spend a night over there, so we drove over and, ah, met with Norman Chapman. And ah, with Ted Bundy, we asked about the fingerprint card, and we asked them to contact the FBI to see if they had any matching cards, and we didn't have ACES, the automatic fingerprint card back then, so you couldn't just put this into a system and get a hit back then. You had to do it the hard way, you had to wake up an FBI agent, they had to take it to the office (*after it was faxed to them*) put it into a machine and send it to Washington, and ah, this is what came back: Theodore Robert Bundy was an escapee; that's how we found out who he was. But prior to getting notification back from the FBI, we went in to talk to him, and we had all the reports from Tallahassee on the credit card cases because we'd gotten the numbers and everything and got the packet together and went in to talk to him. And he admitted to stealing all the cards, and he got lots of them from Sherrod's next door to the Chi Omega house. Ah, he got a lot of them from Publix and Winn Dixie, women would leave their purses sitting in the basket, and they'd go over to get something and he'd slip them out of there. He had a lot of them, and ah, we questioned him, he had Kenneth Misner's ID which he resembled. He told us we were going to be real famous, yeah, (*laughs*) we asked him why we were going to be real famous? So, we had enough counts and everything that by morning he appeared before court (*inaudible*) we had a hearing to hold him and ah, ah, I don't remember what time of the morning it was. From the courthouse to the city jail, which is part of the police department, we went over there and they told us that Theodore Robert Bundy was the guy. We received some explanation that he had escaped from…was that the DaRonch case?

KS: Well, they transferred him from Utah, in fact Fisher (*Mike Fisher*) drove him from Salt Lake City, Utah to, he was in Point of the Mountain prison near Salt Lake City to the jail in Aspen, before being transferred later to Glenwood Springs…he actually escaped twice.

DP: Yeah, the first time he…

KS: Yeah, he jumped out of the courthouse window.

DP: Yeah, and the second time, cut a hole in the light fixture.

KS: Exactly. (*It was a rather large, loose light fixture, and some reports had him widening it.*)

DP: But anyway, it was that morning or the next morning that we found out who was representing him.

KS: Was that Millard Farmer? (*An Atlanta attorney, Farmer could not practice in Florida, but he could advise him*)

DP: Yes.

KS: Now, that must have raised suspicions, as he handled death penalty cases.

DP: Yeah, I forgot which day that he came down. We, you know, Ted I guess, had slept that day, and we slept as many hours, and people were calling and they were waking us up every 20 minutes. Anyway, we're discussing the case and what to do and we get a call, ah, ah, we get a call from Chapman. Ted Bundy wanted to talk to us. So, we put a mic in the room and a recorder outside the door. We sat down and asked what he wanted to talk about. We talked all night long, and that's where this (*inaudible*) credit cards and the next night he talked about, and it's in the court record, he talked about "being like a vampire" that he liked to be out at night.

KS: I know (*laughs*), he was always getting into trouble at night. In Granger, Utah, about 2:00 a.m., when Hayward got him, that's Bob Hayward of the Utah Highway Patrol; brother of Pete Hayward.

DP: (*inaudible*) the handcuffs.

KS: Oh yeah, listen Don, you're not going to believe this, Jerry has that, he's got all that stuff, when he brought it to Louisville, that's how I met Jerry, and I got to bring all that stuff into my house and photograph it. He still has it. He brought it to show Jim Massie (*Patchen knew Jim Massie as well*), and he and Jerry have been friends for over 20 years. Yeah, it was when I first met Jerry when he came to Louisville in 2005.

DP: Well, anyway, I think it was the next day when we got a call from Fisher (*Mike Fisher, and he explained to Patchen who and what he was dealing with, and that he was coming to Florida*), and anyway, once I got some of their papers his MO was always the same (*until*) Chi Omega where he went crazy. We talked with him for 40 hours throughout the different nights, and in the middle of it we were transferred to the Leon County Jail and ah, I mean, and he implied when he ah, was in jail, he felt like he had this problem under control, and ah, you know he thought he was picking a university closer to the water, closer to the coast. And he came here and he went to classes; he had some, ah, soft pornography of any type, basically cheerleader stuff that we found in his car.

KS: You know what's odd about Bundy and Chi Omega, soon after he left Chi Omega, he was seen by a guy carrying that log by his side, and he figured it was about 3:20 a.m.

DP: Well, we figured when I was at Chi Omega, he was doing Dunwoody (*where Cheryl Thomas was being attacked in her duplex*).

KS: That girl was lucky she lived.

DP: Yeah, she would have died.

KS: When you were going over to Pensacola the first time, did you have high hopes that this was going to lead to bigger stuff; that this guy was more than just a credit card thief?

DP: Well, me and Steve Bodiford, had worked together for several years, and we were basically just talking about family, and ah, most of the time, cops don't reflect on things like you see on TV, they like to talk about other things, like on a road trip. We like our peaceful time, our away from work time. Unless we're going to something where we already know something about. Then we would work on the questions and things like that. All we knew is that somebody was trolling around with lights off, captured, that had the VW and all the credit cards and stuff. Neither one of us (*inaudible*) read the reports and we went in there. And I'm sure we did discuss something about him. Half the way over there he was asleep. (*laughs*)

KS: When did it finally settle on you that he was the Chi Omega killer?

DP: Well, after I found out what he was, yeah, and heard the stories about the murders by Lake...

KS: Sammamish, where he got two women in one day.

DP: Right, and the hearing the stories of the bones found in the hills, we started to get excited, saying, you know, he's starting to look pretty dog-gone good, so we're needing to gather all that evidence that we can, and our views started getting real clear and we said someone has to process that VW, and we need to be careful. And ah, ah, we decided to have the VW transferred to Tallahassee into a sealed lab. We then went through a day of hassle because we wanted to take it in a truck, and nobody wanted to give us one because it's against the law and fumes could do this, that and the other. So, we ended up pulling it behind my police car. And on the way back we blew a tire on the VW.

KS: Fisher was with you, wasn't he?

DP: Yes, he was, and what's his name.

KS: Listen, listen (*laughing*), in Larsen's book (*Bundy: The Deliberate Stranger*), Larsen sees y'all by the side of the road, and Fisher says: "That Goddamned Theodore, look at the mess he's gotten us in now!"

DP: So, I had to call a deputy (*Patchen told me he looked like Barny Fife*), and I had to pay cash for a new wheel and rim, and it was a long time before we were back on the road.

KS: And they weren't going to give you the truck.

DP: No, we can't, we put tape all around the outside of the car, as the outside of the car had already been processed, but I didn't want anything disturbing it—it had to be surgically clean.

DP: He told me in one of his last interviews we did here in Tallahassee, and his attorneys were going nuts (*because Bundy wanted to keep talking to the detectives*) and Bundy would say" If I want to talk to them, I'm going to talk to them." It drove us nuts and finally we would go. Finally, we said we don't want to hear his mouth anymore. I mean, he's not going to tell us anything. Fact is, he told us, he asked for a priest, and ah, ah…

KS: In Pensacola?

DP: Yes. So, we talked to him, telling him, "You need to relieve your heart of all this" and he says, "I already have, to a priest", and we're saying once we got outside the room, "who the shit…"

KS: And the priest told him not to talk to you (*laughter*).

DP: Yes, and we said, "Who in the fuck let this guy in here!" You know, we were asleep, and because he wants us at night, anyway, when we get there and we learned some idiot let him in there, and of course, the priest won't talk to us.

KS: No, it's like with an attorney.

DP: Well, I'm sorry, but when the priesthood…somebody tells them of a murder, I mean, how can a priest live with himself.

KS: He, the priest, instructed Bundy as if he were his attorney.

DP: Somebody said we need to get ahold of this guy, but that I shouldn't do it.

KS: Yeah, you might lose your cool (*laughter*).

KS: Did Bundy admit to the credit card thefts early on?

DP: He admitted to stealing the credit cards and the car. Most people will not admit to this (*saying things like*) "They must have been in the car already." But not him.

KS: Yeah, he was only concerned about hiding the murders.

DP: He admitted to going to the FSU theater (*not sure what he means by this; auditorium?)* every day (*to steal*); and the stealing of the tag too, the 11 D 1300.

KS: Can you believe he held onto that tag after killing the Leach girl? Even though, what's the kid's name, Parmenter, and Danny Parmenter wrote down that tag number.

DP: Is that the one in Jacksonville?

KS: Yes, Jacksonville, the daughter of a detective, I believe.

DP: We asked him, you know, about wiping fingerprints out of the car. And then he talked about the Utah patrolman who stopped him, and when he told us how he stopped him, he tried to make excuses for it. He said, "I had a brown satchel, rope, (*inaudible*) pantyhose mask with the eyes cut out, and an icepick (*Bundy's murder kit, more items than were mentioned here*). He did talk about this, and he said they also found a pair of handcuffs. What suspect would carry all that? And he also said "the evidence is there, look for it." And he gave us the impression he couldn't control himself. He didn't plan it (*the Florida murders*) like the others, he had no plan; he had no plans to bury the bodies. He was talking already about, you know, he just totally lost it.

KS: That's what Holmes (*Ron Holmes)* said. When I talked to him, he said, before you would know it was Bundy (*in the past*) but the MO of the Chi Omega killings were not like Bundy's MO.

DP: Ok, one of the questions was "Did you kill the girls at the Chi Omega house?" He said, "I don't want to lie to you, but if you force an answer out of me, I won't lie to you. But no, I didn't kill the girls at the Chi Omega house." Okay, I take that as meaning, I don't want to tell you and lie to you that I didn't go into that house. That's a very strong statement.

KS: It's very odd how he would respond to you all.

DP: First person, most of the time. Ah, I asked him (*At this point the tape is basically inaudible, and this lasts for a few seconds. What did come through is that Patchen explained that the city rented a building to house all the investigators from the Tallahassee Police Department and the Leon County Sheriff's Office. This way they would all be working the same case and that all files would be housed under one roof.)*

KS: He also bit one of the nipples, didn't he?

DP: Ah, the ah, in the autopsy, we discussed at length, we didn't even know at the time, there was only one in the United States that bit their nipple, and we had never heard of that, we were on fresh ground. And ah, the ah, (*inaudible)* who was with us, he didn't know what to do with it.

KS: What can you tell me about working with Souviron (*Dr. Richard Souviron*), who handled the casts of Bundy's teeth for the Levy murder?

DP: When we got ahold of Souviron, and everything, there was something about pouring the casting solution into the wound itself. What we ended up doing was to take a reverse photograph and having it analyzed which brought out the image, or something like that. Souviron is the one who did that, and we ended up working with him.

KS: Is he still around?

DP: He's not even from here.

KS: Oh, he's not even from Florida; I didn't know that.

DP: He's from Florida, south Florida.

KS: Miami?

DP: Yeah...he came up here up here and did it in somebody's dentistry office. As I recall, at the time he was called, ah, (*he was*) like only one of eight people who could do a match like that, you know. I think this was the first homicide in the United States it was used in that got a conviction from it.

KS: Did you all discuss; did you question Bundy about the bite mark?

DP: That is the one thing that he didn't want to tell us, you know, you get Joe Blow and all the crazies that come out of the woodwork, we needed to get some facts that only the killer would know. So, he wasn't telling us things that were specific to the case. Now, if he would have admitted to it; the problem is with getting guilty confessions is that you can't see it, and if you see and the defense gets ahold of it and then they're going to try and say "he took that back later", and they're going to try to get the confession thrown out and you want to stay away from those types of angles.

KS: Were you surprised he was so willing to talk?

DP: Oh absolutely, yeah, as far as the credit card thing, but as far as the talk of, "I had a problem, I know I had a problem, I was in jail, ah, I thought I could control it, I know I belong in jail", you know, we talked to him and said you should be in jail for the rest of your life. The thing is, the death penalty was in question in Florida at the time, and we suggested we could talk to the state attorney's office, work a deal with him on something like that; get his attorneys to talk to the state attorney's office, but he side-stepped all that.

KS: Oh yeah, and can you believe after he got a deal that would have given him life in prison here in the state, he didn't take it? Can you believe that?

DP: Yeah, but can you imagine going to prison for the rest of your life? Being a cop, if I was going to prison, I think I'd rather die. You know, I've heard stories on the news and stuff, rapists, and I would assume that that would be a problem for him.

KS: I guess so. Were you there at the end when he was...?

DP: I sat right in front of him.

KS: Oh, you saw it!

DP: I went and sat in the middle chair, and to the right of me some of the state attorneys, some of the defense attorneys were to my left, some of the families were behind me and some of the news media were behind them. He walked in the door; he sat down. He said, "Hi, Don'.

KS: He acknowledged you?

DP: Yeah, I saw his mouth move, he then said hi to the state attorneys and said hi to the defense attorneys. He would nod, they were strapping him in and he would nod. I don't remember what he said officially.

KS: What did he look like coming into the death chamber?

DP: It was like the same Bundy, ah, that we had talked to at night. Now in court he was different, after he was arrested, he was the top of the show (*inaudible*) and he liked it that way. Ah, some of the people, his attorneys that were told to assist him, told me, he wants the show, he definitely liked the show.

KS: Did that bother you watching him die?

DP: No. I'd seen so much death in Vietnam, watching Bundy go, after all he did, it didn't bother me at all.

KS: Don, when he was executed, do they send two charges of electricity through the body?

DP: Three.

KS: What's this talk of it possibly being a woman executioner?

DP: There's no way to tell…they're behind a wall.

KS: But that's a possibility?

DP: I don't know…I would have pulled it. But I'm sure, yeah, some other investigators, other guys you would talk to, through the whole case, on and on, there's these problems, one person had a heart attack.

KS: You mean the families?

DP: No, the police, you know, the stress of it. I went through it, Steve (*Steve Bodiford*), we all did. Well, I've had cases where, you know, famous around here, something happened, and the chief's calling, the city manager is calling, well, this case brought its own problems, everywhere you walked, everybody wanted to know what happened and finally you had to check out from people, make people mad, saying I don't have time to talk to people and stuff like that; you know, no time to talk (*inaudible*) your friends and coworkers…you walk by them and tell them you don't have time to talk about it.

KS: So that wasn't difficult to watch the execution?

DP: I looked forward to it. No, that didn't bother me. It was a final absolution for me, for this case. And it brings closure not only to the families, but to everyone involved with it. I lived with the bodies, the autopsies, ah, ah, the case every day, day after day, with no sleep, questions, the news media following me around. The stress and strain on family life, ah, you know.

KS: Did you have people call your home?

DP: I had, I'll tell you what, I came halfway home and I pulled off to the side of the road and went to sleep, and a truck went by and rocked my car and I woke up and went on home and slept about 30 minutes and the office called—needed my notes!

KS: (*Laughter*) Thank God they didn't have cell phones, or you'd never have gotten any rest at all.

DP: Well, they'd call you on the radio or your beeper would go off and they'd tell you to go to a phone. Stuff like that, they're not (*phone booths*) on every corner and you had to hunt one down, that's 15 minutes out of my life.

KS: Did you all find out who took a pic of Bundy's body after the autopsy; whomever snapped a picture of him on the gurney? Do you know anything about this?

DP: There were autopsy pictures taken throughout the autopsy; there's always a lab ID technician…

KS: So those are available?

DP: Well, they were given over to the state attorney's office and I have no idea where they're at. There are no pictures at the police department as they were all consolidated at one time (*inaudible*).

KS: What about the actual execution, how is it carried out?

DP: I've been over to Raiford (*the prison*) and they walked me through the proceedings and they shaved his head the day before. They place a sponge (*wet*) and put the cradle cap on, and when they flip the switch, his muscles tense up.

KS: Did they ask you to be there, request you to be there?

DP: What happened, I had a friend that worked in the homicide department prior to that time and since then became a chief of police and now (*2008*) was a director of something to the city—he may have retired by now, I don't know, but his wife worked in the corrections office that had something to do with it all (*the execution*), and he called me and said my wife works over such and such, and that's how I got on it. And after that I got an offer to go to the governor's office and sit with him; and it wasn't the governor that called but one of his people. And I said I'm sorry, I got a better seat. (*laughter*)

KS: What happened after the execution?

DP: They were very professional and they told us, you can talk to the media or just drive off, ah, and I chose to drive off. The man that wrote that book, Larsen (*Bundy: The Deliberate Stranger, by Richard Larsen*) and he called me before I went down there, and he said, "Afterward, are you going to come out front?" and I said "I don't know. It depends on how I feel." When I came out, you know, we put our hands up, and the crowd was cheering, and I looked over and I saw the press, and they (*inaudible)* they looked like leaping sharks, I got in my car and drove home, and he called me at home that night, and he had said, if I don't see you can I call you tonight at home, and I said yes, and he did and I gave my feeling about it, is basically what I told him.

KS: Did Larsen have any comment about it or, as a reporter, did he just listen?

DP: He just asked me, "How'd it go, what did you see, what we did, the whole (*inaudible*)

KS: What was your last meeting like with Bundy?

DP: One of my last times with him, I went to see him and I said, "You know, you struggle in your mind…" I wanted him to talk, and I said, "How can you deal with that, and how many people did you really kill?" and Bodiford left the room, and he said to me, "You know, it's three digits, Don" and ah, I said, "But how do you live with it?" and he said, "Well, you have to look at it, you have to handle it yourself." Well, that leaves you with cold chills. No conscience there at all. You know, it was a sexual thing (*inaudible*) and he couldn't gratify himself unless he did these things. He even had, we talked about his girlfriend, and ah, garroted—strangling—his girlfriend one time, and had ah, he went a little too far, but we found out, I don't know, it may have been Chapman who found it out. (*Bundy used his hands to strangle Liz, and she had to "wake" him to get him to stop.*)

KS: Yeah, that was Liz Kendall, her book, it was only published one time in Washington State. Oh, what is the name of that book, it's Kendall…*The Phantom Prince*, and ah, I asked Keppel one time, how's she doing after all this time, she loved him and didn't know, but Bundy was killing women…it's really messed up, and I was wondering if she had gotten married in the interim.

DP: We tried to get Bundy to talk—good cop, bad cop—but that wouldn't work on him. So we came at it from every angle, even sending in other officers to talk to him, but he was in that nighttime mentality back then. And once he got into talking, he totally changed from all that, and he'd say "I don't have that problem anymore." Acting like a big shot.

KS: I talked to Ross Davis over the phone, and all those years ago, Ross Davis was big in Republican politics, and he was heading some department, and he said, "Ted Bundy could have been anything he wanted to be, because nobody knew about the dark side." But, you know, it was a Jekyll and Hyde type of situation, really.

At this point in the tape, we were talking about the various papers from his case file that I may have wanted to copy, and we discussed each one that he was going through. I wanted to get back and talk a little about his service in Vietnam, as many returning soldiers or Marines from that war went into law enforcement, I believe, in far greater numbers than from previous wars.

KS: When were you in Vietnam?

DP: I graduated in '66 and I was there at the end of '66, '67, I was there 2 ½ years.

KS: Oh, you did two tours. Did you get wounded?

DP: One time. I was (*inaudible*).

KS: Marine or Army?

DP: Army.

KS: A friend of mine, he was over there in 1969, ah, got there three weeks after Tet (*the North Vietnamese and Viet Cong attack on US and South Vietnamese forces in the south of the country*) stationed at Phu Bai, in the Marine Corps, came home and became a cop in Miami for a number of years, and is now in the ministry.

(*At this time Patchen finds an interesting file containing one of their interviews of Bundy, and we pick up his comments and the case file quotes here...*)

DP: Bundy said he'd never been convicted of a crime where capital punishment was so he (*Patchen begins reading here*) "was concerned about the death penalty. Bodiford asked him if he believed in God. Bundy said, "I do, and frankly, I'm a Christian." Bodiford asks, "Do you believe in an afterlife?" Bundy said, "I can't say, no" Bodiford said, "You believe in a heaven & hell type situation?" (*Patchen inserts here, telling me: we're working every angle*) don't even know if there's a natural life, and if there is, I don't know if it's for a length of time." Bodiford, "Do you believe in a being, a creator, superior to us?" Bundy: "I'd have to say (*inaudible*) that that is true." "Do you believe in an absolute faith, that there's no control over your destiny?" Bundy: "Yes, I understand what you're saying, I think Pensacola, where I turned off, but I doubt that was planned (*inaudible*). (*here Patchen quotes from the record as to what Bundy said, and then talks about Bundy's early years*)

DP: "I'm relaxed, like I was last night, the same psychological state exactly. I'm not a 180 degree turn around, I'm not, I'm going in the same direction." My belief at this point is that he's starting to come out from these first few nights, where we had him in his deepest, most susceptible areas. Bundy says he's not afraid to talk. Bundy talked about how his mother and his uncle, Jack Cowell, were playmates. I asked him if he ever stole anything, and he said, "Yeah, on occasion, go to a drugstore, some comic books. It happened once or twice, situation, I didn't have anything to do."

At this time, Patchen retrieves a record in his file that he immediately notices is an original and is signed by him, Steve Bodiford, and Ted Bundy:

DP: Ah, how'd I get this, I shouldn't even have it…

KS: What is it?

DP: It's a waiver of his Constitutional rights, yeah, there's Bodiford's…

KS: Is that a copy?

DP: That's an original.

I thought it would be good to end the interview with Don Patchen, by sharing some of the detective's wisdom as recorded by the *SunSentinel* on June 29, 1986.

Sun Sentinel

June 29, 1986

Sgt. Don Patchen of the Tallahassee Police Department, one of the detectives on the Chi Omega killings, saw Bundy as three distinct but not schizophrenic personalities -- lawyer, sociologist and murderer.

The lawyer Bundy, Patchen said, was a rational being who excelled at "using every loophole you could think of," including firing his public defenders and leading his own defense, to get his way.

The sociologist Bundy spoke candidly about his "problem," never admitting to murders but talking about the murderer's lust so convincingly that the detectives thought he would confess at any moment.

"He said, 'You have got to see that I spend the rest of my life in jail,' " Patchen said.

But, added Patchen: "The deaths in Tallahassee he didn't want to talk about. He just kept saying, 'The evidence is there. Keep digging.' " Shown pictures of Leach, Bundy denied any knowledge of her death.

The murderer Bundy was a conscienceless egomaniac who delighted in outsmarting police, Patchen said. When detectives suggested that Bundy could put the Leach family at rest by confessing, Patchen said Bundy crumpled up a cigarette pack and replied, "But I'm the most cold-hearted son of a bitch you'll ever meet."

CHAPTER SIX

A SEARCH FOR ADDITIONAL ANSWERS IN THE BUNDY MURDERS

Because we're attempting to answer some of those unanswered questions pertaining to Ted Bundy and his murders, and clear up any misconceptions that are hanging over some of these cases, I believe a journey through all of his known murders, as well as some he may have committed, are worthwhile. I will be putting forth various scenarios of what might have happened (or most likely happened), as well as mentioning the less-likely unfolding of events. And while we may not be able to "confirm" what actually occurred, it will give readers a better understanding into our best answers as to what happened to these young innocent women and girls. Lastly, there will be some names on the known list of his murders that I will not be mentioning here. And the simple reason for that has to do with the lack of questions or controversies in those particular murders; no arguments as to what happened to them. Where these questions or controversies do exist, they will be covered here.

But before we take a case by case look at his known murders, I will be sharing a theory concerning one aspect of his crimes that I first spoke about publicly when I was speaking at the Serial Killer Symposium titled *Hunting the Hunters*, that was held at Duquesne University in Pittsburgh in September 2019. That theory has to do with how Bundy started his 1974 murders by attacking in the wee hours of the morning, and basically kept it at night until his bold attack at Lake Sammamish that July. And then, after the fallout about "Ted" and the "VW" at the lake, Bundy returned to nighttime attacks and did not surface again to daylight abductions until April 6, 1975 in Grand Junction, Colorado. It appears certain that this abrupt change was due to his actions at Lake Sammamish and the subsequent public response to these murders.

What follows are the known murders committed by Ted Bundy, and the times in which they occurred:

Karen Sparks (2:00 a.m.)

Lynda Ann Healy (2:00 – 4:00 a.m.)

Donna Manson (around 7: 15 p.m. – sundown: 7:10 p.m.)

Susan Rancourt (10:30 p.m. sundown: 8:00 p.m. He was seen on campus that afternoon)

Kathy Parks (11:15 p.m.)

Georgann Hawkins (12:30 a.m.)

Janice Ott (Lake Sammamish daylight attack)

Denise Naslund (Lake Sammamish daylight attack)

Nancy Wilcox (8:30 – 9:00 p.m. sundown: 7:08 p.m.)

Melissa Smith (10:15 – 10:30 p.m. sundown: 6:43 p.m.)

Laura Ann Aime (Midnight)

Carol DaRonch (7:30 p.m. sundown: 5:16 p.m. Escaped!)

Debra Kent (approx.10:00 p.m. sundown: 5:16 p.m.)

Caryn Campbell (7:30 p.m. sundown: 5:05 p.m.)

Julie Cunningham (9:00 p.m. sundown: 7:12 p.m.)

Denise Oliverson (first daylight attack – afternoon – since Lake Sammamish)

Lynette Culver (noon)

Susan Curtis (Twilight. Sundown: 9:00 p.m.)

Margarete Bowman (3:00 a.m. inside Chi Omega house)

Lisa Levy (3:00 a.m. inside Chi Omega house)

Kimberly Leach (10:30 a.m.)

KAREN SPARKS

At around 2:00 a.m. on January 4, 1974, Ted Bundy entered Karen Sparks' rooming house at 4325 8Th Avenue N.E. in Seattle's university district. It is absolutely certain that until the moment he entered her darkened room, he had killed before (we know Bundy killed a hitchhiker in the Tumwater area south of Seattle, as he mentioned this to Bob Keppel). But whatever murders came before this moment, they were sporadic whose numbers may have been small.

This night, however, was the beginning of a launch into murder that, once begun, would not abate nor take a backseat to the other activities of his life. No, just the opposite would occur. This was the first attack of 1974, and it was just the first of many. Bundy was entering a brand new world; a world where he could murder women and young girls, and everything else in his life: his girlfriend, his political career, even his desire to attend law school, was now just a façade given to the outside world so he could murder when they weren't looking. But for Bundy, his first victim of this new life of murder, Karen Sparks, would not be compliant by dying, and as we shall see, for his next victim, he would need to make certain she would die, for to him, dying was the whole point of it. That, and "possessing" her for a time after death. But that was still several weeks away.

When Karen Sparks (referred to in my book, *The Bundy Murders: A Comprehensive History,* as Terri Caldwell) went to sleep on the evening of January 3rd of 1974, I'm sure everything appeared normal to her. Everything was, in fact, humming along normally. But someone was hunting her and she had no idea of the danger fast approaching.

It seems certain, seeing that Bundy was an exceedingly good planner of murder out in Washington State—the state in which he grew up, loved, and knew so well—that he already knew she lived in a basement apartment, and that the door to the residence was often left unlocked. Without question, Bundy desired to take the surprises out of his life when it came to murder, and he wanted his attacks to go well and as close to perfect as possible. But this attack, besides her not dying, would be different from all the rest:

First, there might not have been sexual contact, which is unusual, and of course, no necrophilia would come into play either. From all we know about this attack, Bundy was desiring only one thing: To murder this innocent young woman who somehow found herself a target. It was lacking all the elements of his future killings, and her death alone was apparently sufficient to satisfy.

What we know is that Bundy so severely beat her about the head, that when she was found still in bed by her other housemates around 7:30 p.m., she appeared dead or near death. Some writers have reported Bundy used a metal bed frame. However, I believe this may be incorrect. It appears from what I have been able to ascertain, that she was beaten about the head with an instrument known as a speculum, and once this ended, he savagely rammed this devise up into her vagina. It is likely that when he left her, he was convinced that her severe injuries would result in her death, and she did come close to expiring. Rushed to a Seattle hospital, she would remain in a coma for 10 days and the hospital for 30. As can be expected, she would not fully recover from her injuries.

No one knows how Bundy felt about her survival. He had done everything he knew to kill her, yet she pulled through. It is my belief that he was both troubled and angry Karen survived, and as he planned his next attack, it was going to be very different. And in fact, what he would do in the early morning hours of February 1, 1974, would be unusual; so much so, that when the truth came out, it would bring a sense of shock to many; including some members of law enforcement.

LYNDA ANN HEALY

In the 25 years I've been writing true crime, I have never learned of an abduction more surreal and unlikely than the abduction of Lynda Ann Healy from her rooming house at 5517 12th Street N.E. in Seattle's university district in the early morning hours of February 1, 1974. While we can't know the exact time Bundy struck, it was probably not before 2:00 a.m., and that window of opportunity would have probably closed around 4:00 a.m.

Some have posited that Bundy knew Lynda Healy, a University of Washington student in her senior year. And even if this is not the case, I'm convinced he knew of her and knew what she looked like. It appears they even shared a class, Abnormal Psychology. They both shopped (as did most students) at a local Safeway store, and she appears to have made purchases on the same day Bundy cashed a check at the establishment. So, there are connections, but how solid they are is up for debate.

As to this particular attack, the scenario that brings the pieces of the puzzle of this murder together, is Dante's Tavern, at 5300 Roosevelt Way, only a couple of blocks from Healy's residence. On the last evening of her life, Lynda went with two of her housemates and a friend by the name of Pete Neil, to Dante's to relax, have some fun and share a pitcher of beer. Just innocent fun. Because Pete had to get back to catch the 9:41 bus back to his place, their time at the bar was relatively short, and soon they would be walking back home.

Unknown to them, Bundy had likely been in the bar and had watched them, and as they left, he probably kept a safe distance from the four slightly tipsy college students. In any event, he was not spotted by them. Later, Bundy would tell a writer (and this had to have been once the house got quiet) that he checked the front door and it was unlocked. He did not enter the premises, but decided to come back later in the early morning hours to do what he wanted to do. So, because this book is about laying out the seemingly endless questions (some important, others not so much) that surround the case and, in one way or another, all of the murders, I will be setting up the scene for each and every location of murder, and we'll tackle the questions from these positions, and I will do my best to answer them, or at the very least, supply you with the best and most likely chain of events that occurred. So, let us now set the scene of the location where Lynda Ann Healy was abducted from her bed in the middle of the night, and whisked away forever.

The rooming house at 5517 12th Street N.E. sits high above the street, and the front door is accessed from the street by climbing two sets of steps. After you ascend the first steps to the home, you are met with a sidewalk that leads off to the right and angles along the side of the home. There is a side door on the right of the house (right, if you are looking at the home from the sidewalk), and it is not located in the center of the structure, but closer to the front of the home. This is also the door Bundy almost certainly would have exited coming from the basement, as it was the quickest way out of the house and into the night. That said, because of what he told a writer about that night (in the usual third-person scenario), he entered the front door of the home because the door was unlocked.

Running directly behind the residence is an alleyway that is somewhat narrow; so much so, that even driving a VW, it would have been difficult to park and leave the vehicle as he could inadvertently block another vehicle, and how would it look if he came out the house with something resembling a body (perhaps wrapped in a sheet or blanket) that could be clearly seen by anyone in that car or truck? When I was there in 2015, I looked for a gate on the fence at the rear of this property and discovered there was none. That alone wouldn't necessarily deter Bundy, as he could simply heave her over from his shoulder, and "drop" her as carefully as possible. I was also told that down the alley and close to this spot, there's a type of alcove where Bundy could have stopped his VW and would have been confident there wouldn't be an issue.

Did Bundy, once he carried Lynda Healy up the stairs and exited that side door, turn right, quickly descend the first set of steps and head for his car? Or did he turn left, and, barring any bushes that engulf the fence today, lay her over the wooden fence and let her fall? While we cannot know for sure (and at this point never will), it appears his wisest choice would be taking Lynda through the backyard and into the alleyway.

The question also arises as to what Bundy did and did not do when he was in Healy's room. Some believe Bundy bludgeoned her with a crowbar or some other heavy object, but the blood evidence (and Bundy's third-person confession to Stephen Michaud,) say otherwise. For one, if you view the pictures taken at the scene, you're met by blood that flowed in a pattern, and not the spatter pattern you would see when a bludgeoning or a beating occurred. In such cases the blood is dispersed into the air and the surrounding area with a velocity not found in a blood flow pattern. In one popular Bundy book, it has Bundy dressing Lynda Healy before exiting the apartment, but that is the opposite of what Bundy told Michaud. Here's a brief exchange between Bundy and Michaud in *Conversations with a Killer*:

SM: I guess you would have to dress her yourself?

TB: I*n that kind of situation a person who was alert enough to be able to dress would not be afraid in terms of struggling or crying out. So it would be unlikely that any attempt was made to clothe the girl.*

SM: Then she was unconscious?

TB: Well, walking out under her own power at that hour of the morning would not necessarily be the soundest kind of approach.

A likely scenario of events for the Lynda Healy abduction can be surmised in the following explanation: As Bundy walked through the front door (and likely using a pen light or a regular flashlight) he made his way through the house, and by chance or by plan, took the steps down to the basement. Walking down the longest portion of the steps, near the bottom (and as you face a wall), you turn right and follow a short section of steps putting you in the basement. At that spot, Bundy had his choice of two rooms to enter, and he chose the one directly across from the steps, which was the room of Lynda Ann Healy. Of course, he likely assumed that the other room was also occupied, so he would have to keep noise to a minimum and rendering someone unconscious quietly could make things problematic. Even so, he entered her room and found her asleep. The authorities believe she was asleep as she (they) made no noise at all, and there was no scream that you'd expect had she seen a man coming towards her. Karen Skavlem, sleeping next door, would surely have awakened had there been a commotion in Healy's room.

At some point, and probably almost immediately after Bundy discovered Healy was asleep, he climbed into her bed, got on top of her, and as he started strangling her, she had to have awakened but was soon so deprived of air slipped into unconsciousness. It is to be noted that Bundy almost certainly did not sexually assault her at this time. Instead, he hung up her bloodied nightgown, either laid her on the floor or in a chair, and made her bed perfectly. He also took a red backpack and some clothes as he prepared to leave. However, because he admitted that making the bed was to throw off police, the backpack and clothes had to be for the same reason. Bundy understood she wouldn't need them, as she was going to die sometime in the next few hours. It was all about creating an image of Lynda leaving in the middle of the night of her own volition, and for a while this was believed by her housemates. They theorized she may have had a nosebleed in the middle of the night and left to have it attended to. But if that was the case (and since she didn't have a car), why didn't she take her bike? Over the next number of hours, however, all of this would unravel as her dormmates, as well as Lynda's family, discovered she was nowhere to be found, and all had that inner sense that something terrible had happened to her.

DONNA MANSON

The abduction and murder of Donna Manson is a case study in preparation (by Bundy), and how both the layout of the campus and the natural environment in which it was built, aided the killer in the abduction of his victim. I will be going over a number of facts pertaining to this abduction and what ruse (if he used a ruse) or type of attack Bundy initiated to obtain Donna Manson. I will also be using information I discovered in 2015 as to the actual site of the Jazz concert she was headed to while I was at Evergreen State College doing research into this murder. That information was published the next year in *The Trail of Ted Bundy: Digging Up the Untold Stories*. And while this information was covered in the book, I did not go into great detail as to what might have happened. But that's exactly what we will do here. What follows is a description of Evergreen State College from my book, *The Trail of Ted Bundy: Digging Up the Untold Stories:*

Carved out of a beautiful forest of fir trees, the concrete complex known as Evergreen State College blends well into its natural surroundings. There is a definite harmony visible there between the ruggedness (and sometimes ruthlessness) of the forest, and the warmth and safety of civilization, something the school has managed to maintain to this very day.

Walking the campus during my 2015 trip, it was evident that little has changed at the school since that March in 1974. The trails weaving their way through the campus offer seclusion at every turn. Even without knowing what happened here, it can easily give a person the creeps if one begins to dwell upon the slasher or horror films they've seen growing up, or if they contemplate the ultimate of horrible realities: the serial killer.

Donna lived in the dorm for first year students in the eastern part of the campus. When I was at Evergreen in the summer of 2015, I spoke with a fellow in archives who actually started at the college in 1974, and because of his judicious searching he discovered where exactly the jazz concert was being held that Donna would be attending. It was being held on the first floor of the library; the very building housing the archives located in a below ground level office of the building.

Donna left her dorm around 7:00 p.m., and her walk would take her on a winding and secluded trail and when she came out on the other end, she'd be in a more open area of the campus and very close to the library. Sundown that night, March 12, 1974, was at 7:10 p.m., so the light was fading as she began the short trek through the tree-encased trail. Her path would most likely have been a winding one and would cover a couple hundred yards, with about one hundred of those yards being encased in thick trees.

We do not know how Bundy abducted Donna. We do know no one reported seeing her, either entering the clearing as she came out of the woods, or outside or inside the library. That tells me that Donna likely disappeared along the trail, and the only question would be is did Bundy waylay her on the trail with his 6577 Sears model crowbar (this was a short crowbar, 18 inches long), or did he convince Donna, through perhaps an offer of drugs, to follow him to his car which probably was parked on a nearby road. If she said yes, that would have been the easiest way to do it. On the other hand, if he came upon her quickly and struck her, he would have picked her up and carried her through a short-wooded section to where his car was parked. But, however he abducted Donna Manson, it was done with stealth, and she just disappeared, seemingly into thin air. And these odd disappearances, where his victims would seem to vanish, was a hallmark of Ted Bundy's murders.

SUSAN RANCOURT

Susan Rancourt disappeared as she was walking on the campus of Central Washington State College around 10:00 p.m. at night, on April 17, 1974. Before we get into what happened to Susan, here's some info from my book, *The Trail of Ted Bundy* that will give you some perspective on what Bundy had to work with that aided him in this murder. He had, in fact, picked the most desolate location on the campus:

The area of Bundy's hunting centered on the Bouillon Library (now Bouillon Hall), which sits between Walnut Street, in front, and Chestnut Street, which runs along the rear of the library. If one stands in front of the library, Black

Hall is on the left, facing the side of the library. Squeezed in between these two buildings was a round structure known as the Grupe Conference Center (still standing today). In 1974, there was a small man-made pond that ran between the conference center and Bouillon, and the bridge spoken of in the record ran over this pond and parallel to the library. So walking this bridge means you're either walking toward the library or away from it, as students could only enter the building through the main front doors. Knowing this is critical to understanding Bundy's movements in conjunction with one of his potential victims, and I'll have more about this shortly.

At one time, the Milwaukee rail line angled its way through the campus, but the railroad trestle Bundy made use of is now long gone. I brought along for my visit a copy of a map of this area that investigators used and on which they had marked locations pertaining to the murder victim, potential victims, and location of Bundy's parked car. At the time Bundy pulled into this area, which is approximately 150-plus feet from the library (and only a slightly bit closer to Black Hall), it was very much a desolate area. The closest building, Black Hall (not the Black Hall of today, where additions have been added, making it appear from the air like an "H" shape rather than one elongated structure), was not giving off much light. And the two parking lots available to students for this area were both north and south of this location and too far away to provide sufficient illumination.

Today, buildings sit all around this location, and the two parking lots have now joined to become one massive parking area, essentially gobbling up this infamous spot. So with the trestle removed and the uninhabited now habited, you must, while standing there, mentally visualize what it must have looked like as Susan Rancourt walked with Ted Bundy to his Volkswagen on that dark night of April 17, 1974.

Bundy had started hunting earlier in the day but had come up empty handed, but that would not be the case with Susan. Just before Bundy encountered her, Susan had attended a meeting for those wanting to become dorm counselors and was heading back to her dormitory at Barto Hall. She had laundry in the dryer to pick up first, but then she'd be back in her room soon after that. But without her knowing it, all that was slipping away from her forever.

As previously mentioned, Bundy had mainly been hunting women around the Bouillon Library, but later in the night, around 9:30 p.m., he was spotted a few blocks south of the library by Kent Barnard (whose testimony can also be found in *The Trail of Ted Bundy*) who'd seen Bundy earlier in the day walking in front of the library with a sling on his arms while trying to carry books. What follows is a brief passage from my book, *The Bundy Murders*:

A little before 8:00 p.m., and only moments before Kathleen D'Olivo would be entering the Bouillon Library for two hours of uninterrupted study, Susan Rancourt placed some clothes into one of her dorm's washing machines and walked to Munson Hall, located at the southern end of the campus, where she attended a meeting for those wanting to be dorm counselors. The meeting was due to end about 10. The last people to see Susan said she was wearing a yellow, short-sleeve sweater, grey corduroy pants, a yellow coat, and a pair of brown Hush Puppies. At 10:15, as Barbara Blair was crossing Walnut Street at Eighth Street (the location of Munson Hall and close to the library, which is also on Walnut), she saw a man "in a green ski parka, who acted as though he were in a daze," as well as a young white female "wearing a yellow coat going north on the Walnut Mall." This was no doubt Susan on her way home, on a path which would take her past the library, where she would turn right, and keeping to the sidewalk between Black Hall and the Bouillon Library, take a left on Chestnut and continue north towards Barto Hall where she lived. She was, in fact, traveling almost the exact route Kathleen D'Olivo had taken a short time earlier. But Susan never made it to her residence. And like Lynda Ann Healy and Donna Gail Manson, Susan Elaine Rancourt appears to have vanished into thin air.

Having convinced her to help him, Bundy would walk with Susan, and just as they started to pass the library, they turned right and walked across the short bridge that stretched across a man-made pond, and as they stepped off the bridge, they angled left and passed the old Black Hall (only one building in 1974), and headed to where Bundy had parked his VW under the railroad trestle that was bounded by high grass. This area was almost pitch-black, with no other buildings around, and there wasn't any reason for students to even be in this area at night.

When Susan first agreed to help Bundy, she learned they were both headed in the same direction, as her dorm, Barto Hall, sits north of the library. In Susan's mind, she knew it wouldn't be any trouble helping him, although we'll never know if she felt any trepidation when she learned where they were going. Even so, Bundy being Bundy, knew exactly how to calm her fears and keep things pleasant and under control until the attack began.

Even though Bundy never talked about how he got her into his car, we know exactly how he did it. Carrying books for him, he hit her in the head with the crowbar as she was bending into the car; or possibly as she was straightening up and was turning to leave. This is exactly what Bundy had done to Georgann Hawkins, Julie Cunningham and Caryn Campbell; however, he used heavy snow boots to knock Campbell out as she was placing crutches into his VW.

Once Susan was knocked out cold, he laid her in the floor area where the passenger seat would be had he not removed it for this particular hunt. And in a bizarre and surreal twist, as Kent Barnard was heading home that night (Kent was a student at another college and had come to CWSC that day to visit his girlfriend; it was also Barnard's birthday) without knowing it, he'd spotted Bundy's VW in the dark and deserted Issaquah hills. What follows is from *The Trail of Ted Bundy*:

Perhaps the most chilling sight Kent Barnard caught that night (though he didn't know it at the time, of course) was during his drive back to Seattle:

"I drove back to Seattle later that night by way of I-90. About 10 miles east of Issaquah I saw a set of small round taillights about 200 yards up a logging road on the north side of I-90."

This would have been Bundy's Volkswagen, containing (no doubt) the unconscious Susan Rancourt, whom Bundy would kill there. Kent Barnard has thought a lot about that day over the years. He's thought about Bundy and his ruse of using the sling. His mind has also drifted back to the small glowing taillights he'd spotted on that deserted logging road, and he's thought about Susan Rancourt. And, I suspect, for the remainder of his life, his mind will occasionally take that journey back to April 17, 1974, and what he saw at Central Washington State College.

KATHY PARKS

Kathy Parks was a student at Oregon State University in Corvallis, and her encounter was a heart-breaking example of how chance and circumstance played a role in her abduction and murder. As Bundy would relate long after his capture, his traveling 250 miles south of Seattle to Corvallis, Oregon to obtain a victim, was all about throwing off the police back in Washington State. He believed that having this type of disappearance happening in Oregon similar to what was now becoming common in Washington State, would have Seattle investigators scratching their heads as to where the killer was located. Things didn't work out that way, but that was his intention nevertheless.

So, when Bundy made that long trip, it is extremely likely that once he arrived on campus, he did not start the hunt for a victim until nightfall. We can confidently say this as (and this was a hallmark of the Bundy abductions), those later interviewed at OSU do not recall seeing anyone who looked like Ted Bundy. And as to his meeting with Parks, no one seems to have seen that either. Or, as I suspect, no one saw anything that led them to believe whatever they saw of the activities of those around them would have led them to suspect something was wrong which also might have sharpened their focus on the two as they were walking to his car. Nothing stood out in anyone's mind; that is, nothing can be found in the official record or testimony that anyone saw anything that night. As such, I wrote about the Kathy Parks abduction and murder based on all the available evidence, and that account can be read in my book, *The Bundy Murders: A Comprehensive History.*

However, I posited two things that might have happened that night, and a year after the publication of the book, I was contacted by the last person to speak with Kathy and she confirmed them. So, what follows is how Bundy obtained her, based on what the killer told a writer in the third person, as well as the known habits, later established by the authorities, of Kathy Parks, and how the mixing of the two—Kathy's habits and Bundy's third-person statements—paint a good picture of how it all unfolded that night. Then, what my contact, Lorraine Fargo, would confirm once we spoke a year or so later.

Kathy Parks would often walk the campus at night, and during these excursions, she would usually leave her room at Sackett Hall and walk the relatively short distance to the Memorial Union Commons where she would purchase something to eat or drink from its cafeteria. When she did this, she would often take a seat at a table to relax, and because these visits were often after 9:00 p.m. and in some cases, much later (it was a little after 11:00 p.m. on the night she disappeared), the cafeteria was often close to being empty, save for a few students milling about or the cleanup crew who would not have been paying special attention to anyone. And it is in this setting that Bundy introduced himself to Kathy Parks while she sat at a table in the cafeteria. But as to what happened inside, that will come later.

What follows is from *The Trail of Ted Bundy* and delves into what happened that night, after which we'll move on to the most likely scenario of what happened to Kathy and where and when it happened. The quotations within the text are from *The Bundy Murders*.

Leaving Sackett Hall, she journeyed down the sidewalk, and just before she reached Memorial Union Commons, she ran into her friend, Lorraine Fargo. What follows is from my previous Ted Bundy book. There are two places where I surmise something might have happened, and, for this publication only, those portions are italicized: (for this, I will reverse the italicization).

"At a few minutes past 11, Lorraine Fargo, another friend, saw Kathy walking alone and would tell police: 'She appeared to be dazed and in a dream.' It was a chance meeting, as Lorraine was on her way back to Sackett Hall after an evening of studying at the library. It was warm and clear that night, and as the two of them stood there, Lorraine listened as Kathy expressed her desire to 'be on her own [and that] she did not want any obligations, and did not want to continue [her] relationship on a permanent basis.' Lorraine, who had recently ended a relationship and could see how depressed she was, asked Kathy to break off the walk and come back to her place so they could talk about it. But Kathy, she said, 'just felt like being alone, taking a walk, and trying to straighten things out in her

own mind.' She also admitted to having skipped her classes that week, and that she had been drinking too much.

"It is unknown exactly when her killer first spotted her. Perhaps it was while she was eating in the cafeteria, and he sat down beside her and began to talk? Or he may have seen her stop and speak with Lorraine. Maybe he'd been following Lorraine and noticed the distraught coed with the pretty, waist-length hair and decided he wanted her instead. *Perhaps he could see the vulnerability in her countenance. No one knows for sure."*

I also surmise in my previous book that the letter she sent to her boyfriend may have been mailed during that walk. Again, from my book: "Because the letter bears a May 7 postmark, it may have been mailed that evening, possibly placed in a mail box just a short time before her disappearance.*"*

Now, what is above in italics (for clarity purposes, reversed for this book) *are assumptions I made based on things I knew about Bundy, and what I believed may have happened. Of course, there was no way to know this for a certainty, so I included it in my book as a possibility only. In my mind, it was a very good possibility, of course, but that was all. And then, about a year after my book was published, Lorraine Fargo contacted me.*

Anyway, it was not until I read the excerpt from Kevin's book that I made the 'library' connection. I couldn't help but notice, in his writing, that in many of Bundy's 1st abductions and attempted abductions, he and his victims were in or near a university library. Well... I had been studying at the library the night that Kathy was abducted, and I did have a slightly strange experience while I was there. "There was this guy who seemed to be EVERYWHERE I was. I had a lot to do to complete my report, due the following day, and I was in 'serious study mode.' When I went to the card catalog, there was a guy standing next to me looking through a different drawer. When I went to find the books on the shelves, he was again, right next to me, searching the shelves. He said something to the effect of 'I can never find what I'm looking for here...'

I pretty much ignored him, having found what I needed, and went to a table to begin working. A few minutes later he came and sat down at the same table, opposite side, a few chairs over. He asked if I had an extra pen, which I gave him. I proceeded to work, and he started to speak again. I said 'Excuse me, but I have a ton of work to do,' and I gathered up my stuff and went to another table. [I believe this indeed could have been Ted Bundy. We can't say absolutely, but given his penchant for hunting university libraries, it is more than possible.]

I was annoyed because I had a lot to do, but didn't think much more than that. It was getting late and they had announced that the library was closing soon. As I prepared to leave, I noticed the same guy, a short distance away. I remember being creeped out enough to take the stairs (in a group of students) rather than the elevator, and making sure I exited the library's front door with a number of other students. I stayed very close to a group headed in the same direction that was slightly ahead of me. They crossed the street right about the time I spotted Kathy. I was very close to the dorm at that point, and there were still several people walking in the vicinity, so I pretty much forgot about 'the guy' and proceeded on to Sackett Hall after talking with Kathy.

"I also didn't realize, until reading Kevin's book, that the letter Christy received from Kathy, dated May 7th, 1974, was ever questioned. Kathy, in fact, had that letter in her hand as we spoke, and I watched her mail it in the small mailbox in front of the Commons just after we parted. The place we met and talked was just across the street from the Commons.... her destination after we spoke was no more than 50 feet away."

As the passage above says, that individual bothering Lorraine may have been Ted Bundy. And frankly, while we'll never know, it probably was him. Keep in mind that a few minutes after Lorraine decided to leave the library, she ran into Kathy and talked for only a few minutes and then Kathy walked up the steps of the Memorial Union Commons for the last time. And Bundy very likely walked inside almost immediately after. The meeting itself was probably over in a matter of minutes and Ted Bundy and Kathy Parks were walking and talking to wherever Bundy had parked his car. As far as where he parked, he was likely close to the Commons. According to what Bundy told the writer, Stephen Michaud, in the third-person, of course, was that Kathy accepted his offer to go out for a drink, but soon after he told her he'd forgotten to pick up his thesis or something and he needed to do that first. Having put her at ease through normal and sensible conversation, it's certain she felt no fear at this time—it all seemed so innocent to Kathy. And Bundy, being so handsome and articulate, must have appeared to her just like a regular nice guy. And having this quality allowed Bundy to capture many women during his time of murder. What a nightmarish shock it must have been when the real Ted Bundy emerged right in front of them, and there was nothing they could do about it.

Once Bundy had Kathy beyond the eyes and ears of humanity, he stopped the VW, took control of her and sexually assaulted her, bound her, and made the long trek north to Seattle. One Bundy writer posited that Bundy may have killed Kathy in Oregon and carried only her head back to Washington State. But that flies in the face of two things: First what we know about Bundy and those things he wanted to do with his victims both while they were alive and an intact body, and also what Bundy himself said about the incident years later. What follows is taken directly from the book, *Conversations with a Killer*:

Had he killed Parks in Oregon; he would have left her body in Oregon. He wouldn't have undergone the extreme measure of transporting a corpse several hundred miles! I mean, we're not talking about cross-town, or from one small town to another within a small geographic area. She was taken to Washington while she was still alive.

And so, we have Bundy transporting Kathy alive (probably already knocked in the head with the crowbar to keep her quiet; bound and gagged), back to his normal hunting ground, and once he was on or near to Taylor Mountain, he killed her. He wouldn't have had a great deal of time, either, if we consider he and Kathy most likely entered his car close to 11:30 p.m., and then by the time he drives to where he stops to sexually assault her, he probably wasn't back on the road to head for home until sometime after midnight. Seeing that it's a little over a four-hour drive, he couldn't have arrived at Taylor Mountain until a little after 4:00 a.m. Sunrise there on May 7, 1974 (her abduction was on the 6th) was at 5:43 a.m.., so whatever he was going to do he would have to do quickly. And since we know that Taylor Mountain was the site where Bundy was depositing the heads only (only the skulls and/or mandibles of Parks, Healy, Rancourt, and Ball were located here), meant that he would (immediately or eventually?) discard Parks' head here, but the bodies of the four are buried elsewhere; possible on Taylor Mountain, maybe on Tiger Mountain, or at another spot altogether. By the time the skull and lower mandible of Kathy Parks were found (along with the others), they were only bleached bones. And it would be a shock to authorities when they discovered that she was there. This is how I summed it up in my book, *The Bundy Murders*:

In what was a surprise discovery for some, the cracked skull and lower mandible of Kathy Parks of Corvallis, Oregon, was also a part of the Taylor Mountain find. Being some 250 miles away from where she was last seen on that warm summer night of May 6, 1974, only added to the gruesome nature of the crime. That the killer reached out so far to claim a victim was yet another example of his unpredictability.

GEORGANN HAWKINS

It's quite clear that when Bundy went hunting on the evening of June 10, 1974, he wasn't very concerned about people seeing him, as long as he didn't see anyone he knew. But even if this happened, it's likely he had an answer already prepared to tell them. That's just the way Bundy planned for such surprises. So, as he prepared to go out that evening, Bundy attached a crude "leg cast" to his right leg, and put a split in the right leg of a pair of pants so he could pull it up and over the cast. He also grabbed a briefcase and a pair of crutches and headed (of all places!) to the university district of the University of Washington. It was likely close to 11:00 p.m. when he started to walk the area of Greek Row, and, as he must have anticipated, plenty of people were still out. As such (and foolishly so) it shows both the confidence he had and the disdain he felt towards authorities whom he believed would never catch him.

And it wasn't long before a witness spotted a woman helping Bundy cross 17th Street, and while he hobbled on his crutches, she carried his briefcase. The woman, however, did not follow him anywhere. Incidentally, Bundy had parked his VW a block away from this location in a gravel parking lot with little light available to those passing by, and this was perfect for what the killer had in mind. Bundy, the planner of murder, was about to be successful once again.

Bundy would continue trolling for a victim in the area, either along Greek Row at 17th Street, or walking up and down the alleyway that runs directly behind Greek Row.

And it would be here, in this narrow and well-traveled alley around 12:30 a.m. on June 11, 1974, that Bundy would encounter the sweet and popular Georgann Hawkins. He first spotted her as she was standing in the alley looking up and talking to someone in a second-floor window of the building on the corner; a building she had entered only a short time earlier to visit her boyfriend for about 30 minutes. What follows is a brief description of this abduction and is taken from *The Bundy Murders*:

Duane Covey, whose second-floor room faced the alleyway, heard the slamming of the back door and jumped up just in time to see Georgann leaving. Covey called out to her, and the two spent the next five minutes chatting, mostly about her Spanish test, now only hours away. As they talked, Covey said they could hear someone laughing somewhere down the alley, and Georgann would occasionally glance in that direction. Later, it would be established that her abductor had watched while she spoke to her friend in the window, so it is very likely this laughter came from him; a gleeful laughter, born out of his psychopathic delight at being able to deprive others of her friendship forever. The two friends bid farewell to each other in Spanish, and Georgann Hawkins continued the short walk to her residence. Covey watched her, he said, for about forty feet as she continued south towards the sorority house before losing sight of her in the darkness. Naturally, he then turned away from his window. Yet had he continued standing there for another minute or so, he would have seen Georgann re-emerge from the darkness holding a briefcase and walking beside an obviously disabled man sporting a leg cast and hobbling on crutches. They would, in fact, pass just below Covey's window as they ambled their way up the alley to 47th, where they'd cross the street, turn right on the sidewalk, take a quick left at the corner, and continue north on 17th for about half a block. Just as they were about to pass a makeshift parking lot, unpaved and without proper lighting, the injured man motioned that his car was in the lot. His vehicle, a light brown VW Beetle, was the only one in sight. Unlike Greek Row, this area was completely devoid of human activity.

Once the two entered this spot, they approached the VW, and as they were standing by the passenger door, Bundy had to have handed Georgann his crutches, and as she was getting the door open and placing them in the car, Bundy picked up the crowbar he'd placed under the right rear portion of the car (the passenger side), and swung it with great force, hitting her in the head. The blow to her skull was of such force, that she came out of one of her shoes, and both her earrings flew off. Bundy did not pick these up at the time but peddled his bike here the next day and retrieved them. Luckily for him, there were no police here, as they were all a block away attempting to gather clues that weren't there.

After quickly lifting Georgann into the car, he sped off and took her up to the hills of Issaquah, where he would spend the next few hours doing things that even when he confessed to her murder, he didn't want to talk about. However, knowing Bundy's penchant for necrophilia, and knowing that he admitted to Keppel that he strangled her soon after he arrived at this rural location, Keppel asked him (because he admitted she was dead), just what he was doing with her all those hours, but Bundy ducked the question altogether. Bundy would also confide to Keppel at the end of his life certain things that only the killer and police knew, leaving Keppel without any doubt that Bundy was responsible for her murder.

Now, if we are to believe Bundy (which, concerning his end of life confessions, we should), he told Bob Keppel that he buried her head fairly close by on a hillside, and gave the best directions he could give under the circumstances. Of course, Keppel was hearing this for the first time 15 years after it happened. And by the time the no-nonsense cop took a crew out there, prodigiously following Bundy's directions, her skull did not turn up. And they couldn't do a "do over" with her killer as he was now dead.

Given this, it's understandable for some to believe that perhaps Bundy lied to Keppel. But if so, to what end? What would be the point of lying? Bundy's only hope of staying alive for a few months or even weeks, was to come up with the kind of information that could be validated by real finds. In other words, it would be far better for him to provide answers that led to results (which he did with Debra Kent) that could tell the world he really was telling the truth. And, Bundy realized, that it was appearing that with every passing hour, that no reprieve was coming. As such, he was grasping at anything he could to stay alive, and he knew only truthful information could help him.

Not to mention that in these final confessions, he was being truthful across the board; and in fact, promised Idaho Investigators Russ Reneau and Randy Everitt that the hour he had with them was not very much, and he told them if they needed other answers to get in touch with him and he would try to answer them, and did so when they came calling again. By this time, and in the short time he had left, Bundy was telling it straight in ways he'd never told it before. So, I'm convinced he was telling the truth about Georgann Hawkins' head, and as such, it remains part of the Issaquah crime scene today.

MELISSA SMITH

There are a few questions, but not many, concerning the murder of Melissa Smith. These questions may never be answered to the satisfaction of all Bundy researchers or students of the case, but that which we may wonder about pales in comparison to what we do know about the murder of 17-year-old Melissa Smith.

It was Friday night, October 18, 1974, and Melissa Smith was supposed to go to a slumber party but the phone never rang telling her to come over. And when she made a call to the girl's home, no one answered. It was looking like the 17-year-old might be in for the evening where she'd be forced to curl up in front of the TV to catch one of the shows on that Friday night's lineup. And what a wonderful outcome that would have been. But the phone finally did ring, and it was one of her friends calling from her job at the Pepperoni Pizza Place, asking Melissa to come up for a while. Happy to get out of the house, Melissa walked out of the door of her home for the very last time. It was dark when she left, but she made it to the restaurant without any problems.

Unbeknownst to Melissa, only a short time earlier, and perhaps while she was talking to her friend, Theodore Bundy was sitting at a bar called Widow McCoy's, where he was having some drinks. He was in hunting mode, and per his usual MO, he was in the process of jump-starting himself into that dark realm of murder through the use of alcohol. Somewhere between 8:00 p.m. and 8:30 p.m., as Melissa Smith was walking out of her house to see her friend, Louise Cannon, a bank teller who knew Ted Bundy as he had an account there, spotted a rather subdued Bundy sitting alone at the bar drinking. Bundy, who liked Louise and wanted to date her, could only say "Hi Louise" after he noticed her. At any other time, he would have chatted her up, and Louise found his present demeanor very odd. After saying, "Hi Ted" she kept walking to her table to join her friends. And the next time she looked over, Bundy was gone.

By the time Bundy left, Melissa was already at the Pepperoni or close to entering it, and at approximately 9:00 p.m., she called home and told her sister, Jolene, that she'd be home by 10:00, and the lives of these two people—one a nice young girl, the other a homicidal psychopath—were about to converge.

Now, when I wrote *The Bundy Murders*, published in 2009, I did not have the story of Louise Cannon, and it would be a number of years before a valid Bundy contact would give me her name so that I could interview her (Louise Cannon's story can be found in my book, *The Bundy Secrets: Hidden Files on America's Worst Serial Killer*). However, once I received it, it presented a clear and terrible picture of Bundy and how he prepared himself for murder. Having these helps a great deal in filling in the picture of the events of that evening. And thankfully, that which was unknown about Bundy that night prior to the abduction of Melissa Smith, is now known.

That said, there are still some unknowns about that night, pertaining to how Bundy obtained her as a victim. What follows is from my book, *The Bundy Murders: A Comprehensive History*:

Her route home would be the same, although there is the possibility she intended to catch a ride part of the way, as at least one witness said he saw her hitchhiking about the time she should have been heading home (when her father learned of this he was quite upset, as he had warned her of the dangers). If this is true, Bundy may have been there to lean over and pop open the passenger door for the grateful and smiling young lady, and that would have been the easiest and the safest way for him to abduct her.

But if she walked home, she did have to cross by, or go over the grounds of a middle school, where there were gaps in the lighting, and it would be near here that a witness, standing out in her front yard at that unlikely hour raking leaves, would hear a scream pierce the night air around 10:15 p.m. If this was the terrified cry of Melissa Smith, then Bundy captured her much as he overpowered Nancy Wilcox, except there is little doubt that from the moment Bundy saw Melissa, he intended to murder her just as he murdered all the others. If he did abduct her during that walk home, it may well have started in the pizza restaurant, with Bundy eyeing her from another booth. Later, after Bundy had been identified in the press, a witness emerged who told police that a person he believed to be Bundy sat in the booth just behind Melissa and exited almost immediately after she left the restaurant. Although it's never been firmly established that Bundy was in the pizza eatery that night, it is very likely he was. Situated close to State Street, a main drag running north and south for miles and filled with hordes of young people cruising in their cars or walking past the shops and restaurants, it's just the kind of place Bundy liked to be.

He could have parked his VW at a spot farther down the street and simply waited behind a tree, car, or some other object, only to jump out at Melissa as she passed by. At that point, she would have had time to utter one terrified scream only. Having his weapon of choice gripped tightly in his hand, a Sears model 6577 crowbar, he quickly silenced Melissa by whacking her in the head with the heavy instrument and dropping her to the ground. It would then take perhaps ten or twelve seconds to place the unconscious girl in his VW and speed away. With a location already picked out, Bundy would have privacy for what he wanted to do. Outside of drawing the attention of one person who saw nothing and thought little of the scream, things had gone according to plan.

Personally (and because the late-night scream was heard in an otherwise quiet neighborhood), I have always believed Bundy did not give her a ride but attacked her much like I described in the book. I have not ruled it out completely that it couldn't have happened another way, as with Bundy picking her up as she was hitchhiking, but it looks far more plausible that he attacked her in that somewhat darkened area, and she had time to let out one scream only. For me, the question of the manner of her abduction is not debatable, as I'm more than reasonably comfortable with the scenario that he overwhelmed her as she walked home. The real question, in my view, is what did he do with her after he abducted her. But before we go there, let's take a look at how and where she was found nine days later. What follows is again from *The Bundy Murders: A Comprehensive History*, second edition, published 2020:

In the early afternoon of October 27, deer hunters came across the body of a young white female on a brush-covered hillside in Summit County, Utah. She was nude, except for a beaded necklace and what appeared to be a man's blue sock wrapped tightly around her neck. These were the only two items with the body. One of the hunters, Phillip Hughes, made a call to Summit County Sheriff Ron Robinson. But Robinson, short on manpower, asked for the assistance of the Salt Lake County Sheriff's Office.

At approximately 4:00 p.m., Detectives Ben Forbes and Rick Sommers arrived, as did their superior, Captain Pete Hayward. Detective Forbes's report describes in clinical detail the condition of the body before them. "The location of the crime scene is approximately due east of the Summit Park subdivision, bordering Timberline subdivision. The actual area of the crime scene itself is mainly predominated by fairly heavy scrub oak and innersparsed [sic] small pine trees. In some fairly tall scrub oak the body of a white female ... present age unknown, appears to be about 5'4" to 5'5" ... 110 to 115 pounds, auburn-reddish hair. Around the neck of the victim is a necklace made of wooden beads.... Also around the neck of the victim is what appears to be a man's navy blue knit sock, and this is tied behind the neck of the victim."

"The body is located on its stomach," he continued, "with the left arm completely folded underneath the body and the right arm extended and unfolded at a 90 degree angle and both legs bent at the knees." Forbes goes on to note the heavy abrasions on the shoulders which continue down the back and the cuts and abrasions on the buttocks

and legs; although he doesn't state it in his report, these are post-mortem injuries caused by dragging the remains over rough terrain.

Squatting down, Forbes leaned forward to get a closer look at the damage to the head, and notes that besides the obvious blunt-force trauma she'd suffered, "approximately 6 inches above the top vertebra is what appears to be a bullet wound of contact." But of course, there had been no bullet fired through the head of Melissa Smith. The extensive damage done to her skull had been the result of the blow from the crowbar only. If the veteran detective could have at that moment miraculously examined the craniums of the murdered women of Washington State, most of which were yet to be discovered, he would have recognized the similarities right away.

But perhaps the most stunning discovery of the day was the determination of the time of her death. From the condition of the body, Forbes believed she'd been dead for no more than thirty to thirty-six hours. But even if you were to double that time, it meant that Melissa Smith had been held at a location for the pleasure of her abductor for at least five days; very likely in a state of unconsciousness the entire time due to the head injury. It is my contention, based on the theory of an investigator from Colorado, that he kept Melissa, as well as upcoming victim Laura Aime, either in his upstairs apartment at 565 First Avenue, or down in the cellar, the entrance of which is located in the rear left-side of the home. Indeed, he may have used both locations. Here he could clean them, make love to them, and prepare them for their trip into the wilderness where he would finally release them for natural decay.

So, it's clear that Melissa Smith was kept somewhere alive for a number of days. When I was working with the Colorado investigator, Mike Fisher, he said he believed that "Theodore" (as he would always call Bundy), had kept Melissa Smith somewhere on the property at his rooming house at 565 First Avenue, and Fisher thought it might be in the utility room, as Bundy was acting apartment manager/groundskeeper, and could have easily done so. Because the utility room was not, in my mind, the best place to keep a victim due to its size, I believe the most likely location was inside his room. And if you look at the Lynda Ann Healy abduction, where he carried her up the steps in the middle of the night, went out the side door and carried her to his car—all without being seen—it's more than plausible he could have done this (both up to his room on the second floor, and down again days later) in the middle of the night, and each trip would have only taken him two minutes or less. I stated that while it can't be proven, it's likely it happened.

And then, a number of years later, I was made aware of a cellar located (if you're standing in front of the house, looking at it) to the left of the house and in the rear. And one of the residents who knew Bundy said that he could hear Bundy down there making noise at all hours of the night. Add to this that the cellar was covered by a top that had a lock to which Bundy had a key, then this would be the best place to keep victims; especially victims he had for only a short time. And in fact, during his end of life confessions, he told Utah detective Dennis Couch that he kept victim Debra Kent up at his apartment for one day before disposing of her. And while he said apartment, I'm assuming he meant apartment grounds and not literally the upstairs apartment. It would just make sense to have her here in this cellar for the short duration.

But what about someone like Melissa Smith, who remained alive for a number of days, likely in a coma. Would he have kept her in that dank cellar for nearly a week? Perhaps not. I was informed years ago that while Bundy normally kept his apartment in Utah unlocked, there were occasions when others found it locked. Why the change? Perhaps he had a victim there, and in the comfort of his home, he could do those things he enjoyed doing, knowing he could quickly get rid her of at any time by simply doing with her as he had done with Lynda Ann Healy. And the moment we say "he would never do that" we'd be missing the essence of who Ted Bundy was: he was an arrogant individual who believed he could get away with anything—including murder—as the law enforcement community was just too stupid to catch him. Add to this that Bundy loved the thrill of living on the "edge", willing to perform some of the boldest abductions on record, be it in front of hundreds (Viewmont High School) or even thousands (Lake Sammamish), then you have a man who would absolutely use his apartment to keep victims for a while so that he could do things to them. So, as I see it, I believe he absolutely used the cellar but, in my mind, he used his room as well (see, "Did Bundy Keep Victims in His Room", in this book). It's just the thing Ted Bundy would have done.

As can be expected, Chief Louis Smith and the family never recovered from the loss of Melissa, and the chief passed away in 1985 (four years before Bundy was executed). Melissa's sister, Jolene, who told Colorado investigator Mike Fisher that when she saw the body of her sister, she noticed Melissa was wearing a brand of makeup she never owned (giving rise to the theory her killer had done this), died in 2014 at the age of 55.

LAURA ANN AIME

I'm including Laura Aime in the mix in this book due to a certain question (which is a very important one) surrounding her murder as to when it occurred and how long Ted Bundy kept her alive, and where, before she either expired on her own or Bundy killed her. And in this regard, her experience may indeed mirror Melissa Smith's ordeal with the killer.

But first, here's a brief passage from *The Bundy Murders* revealing how she became a Ted Bundy victim:

On the night of her disappearance, Laura had gone to a party at a house in the suburbs of Orem, less than ten miles north of American Fork. According to witnesses, Laura left the party alone around midnight with the intention of hitchhiking into the city of Lehi and would naturally have taken U.S. Highway 89 going north. Indeed, authorities would come to believe that Laura disappeared along one of the more desolate and dark portions of this highway. Even so, she would have felt no trepidation at the thought of hitchhiking this road, even at midnight, and the warning of her mother was probably long forgotten. Here is where the trail goes cold. As Laura Ann Aime stepped out into the frigid air that Halloween night, she was wearing blue jeans, a sweater, and a hooded coat resembling, authorities said, a navy pea coat. At first glance, it seems almost inconceivable that Ted Bundy could have been in this unlikely location, at that hour of the morning, and so far south of Salt Lake City. But Bundy was nomadic too, and while Laura was learning to stretch her wings, and was in that process of finding herself, Ted Bundy knew exactly who he was and what he was looking for. As Laura slid into the passenger seat and began the usual banter, it wasn't long before the crowbar came crashing into the rear of her head. Like all the women before her, Laura Aime would soon be immortalized in that heartbreaking litany of those who succumbed to the deviant desires of the serial killer known as Theodore Robert Bundy.

I remember years before I decided to write about Bundy, I was sitting with my friend James Massie in a restaurant here in Louisville and we were talking about Bundy, as Jim was good friends with Jerry Thompson (the Utah detective who pulled Bundy out of the shadows), and he was also friends with Ron Holmes, the criminologist, who had interviewed Bundy and exchanged correspondence with him. So, as we talked (and because Jim knew I had an interest in the Bundy case), he allowed me to read copies of all the letters Bundy had written to Holmes. He also allowed me to view the crime scene photos of Laura Ann Aime; photos that he obtained from Holmes (who'd made him copies) that were originally obtained from the investigator that had worked the case. Anyway, the shots of Laura's face and neck, with the ligature still tightly wrapped around her neck causing her tongue to protrude from her mouth, are extremely graphic.

But as we talked and Jim mentioned that she was abducted on October 31, 1974 and wasn't found until November 27 (28 days later), I remember thinking that her body basically showed no decomposition at all. Not only that, but temperatures were quite normal for that time of year (certainly not cold enough to freeze and preserve a body), and so I found it completely strange as to why she looked so "fresh". Bundy had placed her body close to a hiking trail where he had to have known she would be quickly discovered. Here's what I wrote about this in *The Encyclopedia of the Ted Bundy Murders*:

On Halloween night of 1974, Laura Ann Aime (1957-1974) left on foot a party in the city of Orem, Utah, and after stopping to purchase cigarettes, started hitchhiking on what police believed was one of "the darker portions of Highway 89." It would be in this area that Ted Bundy would stop his VW and give young Laura a ride. Here the information goes dark, and her body wasn't discovered until Thanksgiving Day, November 27, 1974. Bundy, who had a habit of occasionally leaving bodies close to roads where they might be easily found, did so with Aime. Around 9:00 a.m. on that cool sunny Thanksgiving morning, two Brigham Young University students parked their car in the lot of the Timpanogos Visitor Welcome Center and headed out on a hiking trail. After going about 500 yards, they spotted the naked body of a female lying just off the roadway. The startled couple ran back to their car and drove straight to the Ranger station to report what they'd seen. The body was that of Laura Aime.

Now, it would be years before I talked with Colorado investigator Mike Fisher about Laura Ann Aime, and it was Mike who first stated that he believed Bundy had both Laura Ann Amie and Melissa Smith at his apartment at 565 First Avenue in Salt Lake City, Utah.

And so, I believe that without question, Bundy kept a no doubt comatose Laura Aime on his property at 565 First Avenue, and there were two options he had: One, she could have been held in the cellar of the apartment (it was in the rear of the complex, and it had a locked covering to which Bundy, as apartment manager, had a key), or he may have pulled what I call a "reverse Lynda Ann Healy", and carried her up the steps in the middle of the night, and carried her back down again—also in the middle of the night—at a moment of his choosing. Either place falls into the realm of possibility, although I think we can absolutely say the cellar was positively used while the room remains a high probability, given Bundy's strange penchant for extreme risk taking. Keep in mind too, that at the end of his life he admitted to Utah detective, Dennis Couch, that he took victim Debra "up to his apartment" where he kept her for one day before disposing her body near Fairview, Utah.

So, as amazing and bizarre as it sounds, it appears he had Laura alive and likely unconscious, for over three weeks before finally killing her. And while it's true Bundy did not talk about that aspect of these two Utah abductions (Smith and Aime) all the evidence points to this being the case.

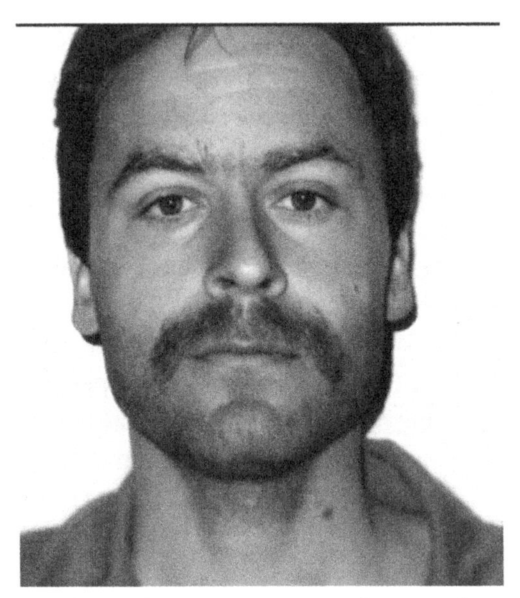

Ted Bundy's 1978 Pensacola Mugshot

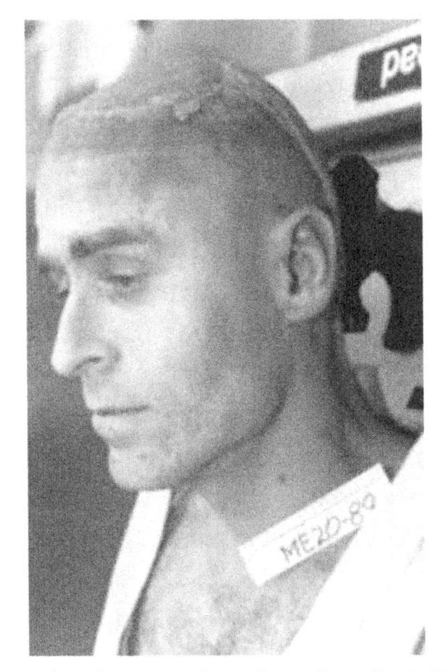

Bundy, deceased in the Florida ME's office, January 24, 1989

CHAPTER SEVEN

TED BUNDY'S UTAH CONFESSION

Because I've taken the time to transcribe the Don Patchen, Jerry Thompson, and Ronald Holmes interviews, I'm taking the time to transcribe Ted Bundy's Utah end-of-life confession. For years this wasn't available to the general public, but since it was released by Dennis Couch, the Utah detective who interviewed Bundy at the end, I've listened to it at least four times. The conversations are not always easy to hear, and there are occasional "dips" in the recording. Add to this Ted Bundy's extreme exhaustion, and how at times he seems to be fading out of the conversation (one or two times he apparently fell asleep), and you have a potpourri of difficulties gauging everything Bundy was saying. That said, that won't be a problem here as a transcript is thankfully continually the same—if I can get the words onto the printed page, you'll get to see them all. However, I urge everyone to seek out the actual recording which can be found on YouTube and likely other sites on the Internet, as there's nothing quite like hearing it all in Bundy's own voice.

It is important to note as well, there are various places on the tape when others are speaking and asking questions. These people are not identified. However, a number of them may be prison staff, or possibly members of Bundy's team. In any event, I will note these as staff or otherwise where necessary.

Lastly (and perhaps for the first time since he became a killer), there will be a moment where Bundy expresses what appears to be a sincere regret for the murders and what he had done to all the families; while making it clear to Det. Couch he's not saying he's sorry for himself.

DC: Today's date is January 22, 1989. The time is approximately 7:30 p.m.. I'm at the Florida State Prison, going to interview Ted Bundy.

TB**:** I want you to know, that uh … we'll do what we can. And I think we can do something good. We can do something good.

DC: First of all, I want to tell you I appreciate the time that you've given me, and another thing a good friend of mine … and an old acquaintance of yours wanted me to tell you he's thinking about you and…

TB: Sure. I remember, is he still at the prison?

DC: No, he's got the county jail, and he's up at the VA hospital. He married myself and my wife back in '76, and my wife died, and he buried her.

TB: Hmm. He's a fine gentleman, I appreciated his work at the prison.

DC: Yeah, regardless of a person's religious beliefs, he's a heck of a man.

TB: Absolutely.

DC: But I've got 5 cases that ah we know of, that we're concerned about. Three of them are missing girls. Would you feel more comfortable just talking, or would you like to have me to refresh your memory?

TB: No, what I'd like to do, I mean, under the circumstances … I think we need … I'd just like to, let's just get a map out.

DC: Unfortunately, I don't have a map of Utah.

TB: Alright I think … guess what … let's just see what we have.

DC: The best I can do … Ok, here we got … of Salt Lake City.

TB: Shit. I knew it …

DC: Not a good enough map huh?

TB: No… it's just… everything looks the same. It used to be a problem back when I lived there. Dammit.

DC: Well there was Debbie Kent up in Bountiful at the high school. Do you remember, did you go north or south or straight east from there?

TB: Well let's … let's try to …. that's what I'm looking for here.

DC: Ok. Well Bountiful is just north of Salt Lake and south of Ogden here. Are there any particular landmarks that you recall, or …?

TB: Well … alright first of all. You'll have to forgive me, because I'm not thinking very clearly here, there's a number of things we need to talk about, and we're going to get down to business here. Ah, I understand, and it's my preference, that you at least for the time being, more or less work in a statewide capacity you know, even though I'm sure you're interested in everything that happened in Utah. But I understand that you've sort of been associated with the Attorney General's Office in some way for this.

DC: Well I've been informed, I talked to the Attorney General today, and he's informed me he's empowered me to act on his behalf as a representative of the AG.

TB: Ok and I would like your findings here reported as soon as possible to him.

DC: You want me to report my findings to him?

TB: Well I can't order you to do anything….

DC: No, I'm saying you'd like me to do that … sure I'd grant that … in fact he asked me to.

TB: As soon as you can, let him know what's going on.

DC: Absolutely.

TB: Now … I know … well I don't know …

DC: If I can help you out. You remember where Carol DaRonch got away from you.

TB: Oh, I know where things are.

DC: I thought that might help you think through it.

TB: I know where all this stuff is, I'm pretty familiar with the map. To a point.

DC: I agree, you weren't familiar with the area, and there are a few canyons…

TB: I think what we need is topographical stuff, for the high resolution, to give me a better feel for that.

? Could not come up with one of those in Starke, they do not have them of Utah.

TB: I know, I know, and that's a problem. I want to be, for any number of reasons, I want to be as specific as I can be.

What this is about is trying to locate the remains. We're not talking about stuff thrown out of the windows, or stuff scattered across the ground. It's things that should be there.

DC: Was it a burial?

TB: Yes.

TB: … in some ways more deserved ….

DC: How far do you think you had to drive from that school?

TB: It was somewhere between … let's just … uh …

DC: Did you go back down through Salt Lake again?

TB: Oh yes, yes.

DC: Oh, did you? And you went further south? Past Provo?

TB: Yes.

DC: Were you on the interstate?

TB: Yes, on the interstate. We're talking somewhere between Milburn and Manatee. Maybe Mayfield. That's a big hunk. An awfully big hunk. You could spend several lifetimes looking for something there. I'm trying to narrow it down. I mean, it's … somewhere … to the left of 89.

DC: You went down the highway as opposed to the freeway?

TB: Right. I don't know what it looks like in the daytime, that's another problem. Mountainous … area, to the east all the way down 89 from Thistle to Mayfield.

DC: So, you went south of Provo down the freeway and then you jotted off onto 89 is that right? Did you follow 89 all the way down?

TB: No no … there's a standard … I think the most efficient way is if you're going for instance to Price you just head down the freeway and there's a turnoff, a turn off for 50.

DC: Yeah, I've traveled Price Canyon … it's called Spanish Fork but it's on the way to Price. But then you took the cutoff at Thistle?

TB: Exactly whether it was a cutoff, whatever was the most efficient way was during those days and it may well be different.

DC: No, it's the same way. There's a cutoff at Thistle and then it goes south. How far south did you go from there?

TB: Look, again, jog over to Thistle and down 89 here, and that's the $64,000 question …

DC: You're stuck?

TB: Well, not necessarily but … we're not … we don't have a lot of detail to work with on this map.

DC: How far down do you think from that cutoff do you think? How many towns you had to go through before you went up into the mountains?

TB: No, I think what we may have to do is work, with not so much time. I didn't count towns, or miles, or look at my watch to see how long the time was, I was just driving, in the dark, late at night, and not very conscious of much of anything else, you know. I don't know what was going on except for looking for a side road.

DC: Let me ask you another question before you lose your train of thought, we have reported to us that there was some carvings in trees … did you ever carve your name in a tree?

TB: Never.

DC: Ok because I think there was one down in that area someone carved the name Ted Bundy and put a date on it … we think three or four of those trees, in different mountain areas. That wasn't something you did?

TB: No, no.

DC: Ok, so we're going south of Thistle, anything come to mind there that you can see on the map that would help us out?

TB: Not on the map. I would have to go on my recollection. I mean of, whatever, um, landmarks I saw.

DC: How about Nancy Wilcox. Are they all down in the same area?

TB: No. Ah, let's try to do one at a time. If I can't do this one …

DC: Ok.

TB: Yeah, I was just hoping we'd have something … this will give us a start … but I was hoping that we'd have something to really clue me in, high degree of scale showing dirt, dirt roads, that would closely clue me in there. But anyway, we're talking about a small town, how small I can't tell you, how big. It certainly wasn't Provo, but it was one of those small towns along here. It was late at night so the stoplights were turned off or at least blinking or something like that.

DC: They have those flashing amber lights?

TB: Yeah. How many of them there were, I don't know. At some point …

DC: And then you went off into the mountains from that small town, the area of that small town?

TB: Turn left, right.

DC: How far away from that town would you have gone?

TB: Several miles. Well, this should help. There seemed to be, just on the outskirts of this town, an iron barrier, a, a gate, that's thrown across the roadway. Looked like it closed off that road for some reason.

DC: Like a cabin association, or something like that?

TB: Possibly. But it was still a paved road, it just looked like … it wasn't closed, but it looked like it had been opened and closed.

DC: How far away from highway 89 would you say you ran into that?

TB: Well again just from the outskirts of this small town traveling up into the mountains east of there …

DC: In terms of ah time, can you estimate how far from Thistle you would have traveled?

TB: No. Absolutely not able to do that.

DC: So, you couldn't do it in terms of miles or time.

TB: No.

DC: Did you return back to Salt Lake all the same night?

TB: Yes.

DC: Was she already dead?

TB: Yes.

DC: Was she killed right there at the school?

TB: No.

DC: But you are responsible for her death, though?

TB: Yes.

DC: Of course, Melissa Smith, we recovered her body. Did you not have time to bury her, or was it just not your intent to bury her?

TB: Can we just try … I want to focus on one at a time.

DC: Ok. Well I'm concerned about the 30 minutes too … is that firm, or what?

TB: Well I'm just, just about ready to collapse. I know that's the furthest thing from your mind. But I've got some mileage left in me tonight, and I want to give it my best … the one that's most likely to produce something for somebody. And this is my clearest recollection. The one that I have the clearest recollection of, and ah, that's why I'm starting there.

DC: From the iron gate then, how far would you say you traveled from there?

TB: Ok, now, at that time, there was a big scene, just a short distance inside the iron gate, to the left.

DC: So you somehow you were able to go through the gate?

TB: Yeah, the gate was open, or partially open. My recollection is it wasn't all the way open or all the way closed. Just closed enough for it to be evident that it was there.

DC: Did you park your car and then carry her through there?

TB: No, it was big enough to drive through, I was driving a Volkswagen.

DC: It wasn't that rough for driving your VW, I mean, it wasn't that mountainous?

TB: No, no, no, no, a short distance, a matter of yards, to the left, inside of that … and I hope that I'm recalling this clearly. There was a dirt road, that made a steep climb, I mean a short, a steep ascent up a little incline, and wound up to the left. Wound around up and to the left into a wooded area. You know, I'm not talking about a heavy forest, but you know the type of woodlands that you find in that area, it's a sort of clump of trees here, clump of trees there, a lot of open dirt, grassy stuff, and you know, that kind.

DC: Were you into the pines, or just kind of the quake's?

TB: Again, the darkness limited my ability to perceive all of that. I mean I knew that kind of country that's the reason I'm describing it to you. A more detailed description I don't have. Ah. And I can kind of remember … I'm trying to remember … the number of little turns this road made and how far up it traveled.

DC: But you're still able to drive it in the VW?

TB: Well it's bumpy, you know it's tough, it's rocky.

DC: Is it a county type road, or is it just the kind you can get one car in?

TB: It's the one car type, back road, saying back road that's not good enough, four-wheel type road, wagon wheel ruts, puddles, deep…. you know a VW is amazingly agile, even in country like that, and so it's even with the deep holes and rocks and things, rocks are around quite a bit if you get up there. It's a covered wagon type road if you will, a four-wheel drive type of road, nothing fancy, something people would get into the back country on.

DC: How far past that iron gate would you say you traveled before you finally stopped?

TB: Traveled very slowly. Bouncing around, you know … A mile to two miles at the outside. I know that's a lot of ground, but then again, uh …

DC: It's hard to tell when you're going so slow.

TB: Yeah, it's hard to tell, and to see it, is one thing, and to try to estimate it and describe it is another.

DC: Did you see any power poles, power lines residences, cabins?

TB: There was … well, a certain point, I did pull off at the side of this road, let's say a mile, roughly. And ah, to the left-hand side, there were remnants of old barbed wire fence posts, and maybe shreds of barbed wire. It wasn't an actual fence, it was the remnants of a fence and I noticed a couple of fence posts kind of bent down, bent askew, and I stumbled over a piece of barbed wire buried in the sandy soil here and there.

DC: Did you stop the car in the road itself?

TB: I believe I pulled off, you know, five feet or something.

DC: Now, then I assume you had a shovel and how far would you say you were?

TB: Let's say, approximately 20-30 feet off the road, let's say 25.

DC: How deep was the grave?

TB: Approximately 3 feet. Yeah, 2-3 feet maybe.

DC: Did her clothes remain with her?

TB: No.

DC: Did you discard those before or after you left her there?

TB: Trying to remember … I don't clearly remember. I don't have a specific recollection. I think what happened was, is that ah, yes, they were cut up and deposited along the side of the roadway.

DC: On the way back home?

TB: Hmm. You know … It's interesting you should say that. I was going to say something else, but … yeah as a matter of fact. On the way home back to Salt Lake City from this point, along the, along highway 89 even down as far up as past Thistle.

DC: You cut 'em up into pretty small pieces?

TB: Yeah … a 3-inch square type.

DC: What was the means ah …. how was she killed?

TB: This is harder stuff to talk about.

DC: Not the nice part.

TB: Well, there are no nice parts. Hard to make judgments of quality here … It's simply more difficult to discuss this.

DC: Did you use a weapon on her? Did you use, manually? Or …?

TB: Um (very long pause) that's why it's so much easier for me to try to locate the body than it is to talk about the actual thing. Ah, just so much more positive, as much as it can be.

DC: Where, um … if it didn't take place at the schoolyard, did it take place in your car, or …

TB: No, the place where I lived.

DC: Oh, you took her home?

TB: Right.

DC: How many places did you live, I know you had a place up in the Avenues, is that the only place you ever lived in Salt Lake?

TB: Oh no, the Avenues…

DC: Up by the university?

TB: Right, right, the Avenues, the name eludes me. The name of that location didn't ring a bell at first.

DC: Would it have been the residence which we searched?

TB: Right.

DC: Well we can talk about that later …

TB: Yeah it was at the residence.

DC: So, did you take her to your residence then down here all in the same night? Or did you keep her for a period of time?

TB: I did keep her there for a period of time. A couple, well, a day … 24 hours.

DC: Ok. Was she alive during that time period?

TB: Well let's see. During half of it. With reference to the things that went out the window, some of the larger items went out between Spanish Fork and Thistle. There's an embankment there where the river comes down. I think there's a railroad track in there somewhere too.

DC: Right, there's been a big landslide, maybe you saw in the news, it was nationwide, a year or two back that whole side of the mountain slid down.

TB: I heard about it. Was that the area?

DC: Yeah that was right there at Thistle.

TB: Well this would've been down from it, it's been a long time. I'm sure there would be nothing left to find, in terms of just stuff cast off the roadway. But I'm concerned about which one of these roads it is. Do you think that's… I wonder, do you think that's enough?

DC: It's going to be very difficult.

TB: Is there any … don't you have any access to maps? It's going to be very difficult, if you don't have maps.

DC: Well I'll do my best to leave here and find a better map. If I can get some time to come back here tomorrow evening, if that's possible.

TB: Tomorrow, there's just nothing open at all. Uh… because what I'm talking about here are, in all likelihood, is remains that can't be found. There's no absolute certainty, but there was an attempt on my part for example to fill in part of the grave and a layer of heavy rocks over that and dirt over that to prevent the kind of ah, animal destruction that can occur to something left …

DC: You were concerned about animals NOT getting to it?

TB: Yeah not getting to it, because well they could conceivably spread the remains around in such a way that they'd be found, as opposed to not being found.

DC: Was she in any way dismembered or was she buried whole, or? …

TB: Yes, you should find all of it.

DC: Well then again, I don't mean to rush you but I'm concerned about getting everything in as much as I can. There are two other gals who are missing and ... Further up there was Nancy Baird who worked at a gas station, July 4th?

TB: Yeah …

DC: That was in '75, July 4th. What, what, do you recall what type of place it was she was working at or where it was located, on which highway?

TB: No, I didn't have anything to do with that.

DC: Nancy Baird?

TB: No, I don't know anything about that disappearance. I…

DC: Nancy Wilcox lived in Salt Lake City on the east side. She had left home. Do you recall where you picked her up?

TB: Uh …

DC: What others did you take down highway 89?

TB: No one else.

DC: Was Nancy Wilcox on foot, or ah, how did you run into her?

TB: Uh, she was on foot.

DC: Did she come peacefully with you, or did you have to take her by force at first, or how did that particular encounter occur?

TB: Oh, uh …

DC: You haven't slept for a while have you?

TB: Well I just … well, there's just a lot of things going on besides what you want to talk to me about. And it creates a lot of pressure, and the lack of sleep and it all builds up.

And it's maybe hard to appreciate… and I've only talked to folks from Idaho today, and it's hard to appreciate, I'm not using it as an excuse but it's just the reality that when I talk about this kind of stuff it just drains me in a way that's hard to describe. I mean haven't thought about these kinda of things… to attempt to relive them vividly enough to describe them especially to the point of locating remains, it just… my, my mind is tied in knots right now. Everything together… I'm having a hard time thinking. I'm having a hard time. Let's see if we can't run through it, at least this one.

DC: Do you remember approximately where you encountered Nancy Wilcox? Do you remember what she was wearing, what she looked like?

TB: I don't remember exactly what she was wearing. She was wearing like, casual clothes. She wasn't wearing a dress, she wasn't dressed up in slacks or a dress. Jeans. Walking along the side… of a road. Poorly lit area. Suburban. I, years ago I probably knew the street name, but on the outside chance I could show you, you don't happen to have a street map of Salt Lake?

DC: No. Do you recall where from the university, say?

TB: Oh, it would have been south. Considerably south.

DC: East or west or?

TB: Oh, excuse me, south. I get my directions all screwed up with that place. Is there a Salt Lake map here…?

DC: Of course, when you're going south, the Wasatch Mountains are to the east. And there's homes built up alongside of the valley—

TB: Oh, it would've been south of the university. Some distance south.

DC: And you remember State Street, the main drag, that goes all the way through, was it east or west of that?

TB: Oh, it was east, south and east.

DC: Considerably east?

TB: Well considerably east is up in the mountains, up in the benches. This wasn't up in the benches. This is uh, south and east, by how much, is just a.... by suburban I mean, I don't mean new suburban, it looked like older suburban. You know, houses been around for a while, wasn't a new development. There were no sidewalks per se, I think it was just sort of a side area. There were no like storm sewers, curbs, anything like this.

DC: Were you able to have any conversation with her?

TB: Not really. (pause) Ah, not much. I mean nothing, nothing noteworthy.

DC: Was she carrying a purse, do you recall?

TB: Don't recall. Well, let me think. Well yeah, you know, you asked me that question about Debra Kent—

DC: About the purse?

TB: About what she was wearing and everything you need?

DC: Well you just indicated what you did with the clothing but you didn't describe it though.

TB: Well, hey... ok. I would hope we get something that could be corroborated in a way that people are semi-convinced. I hope people don't think I'm making it up, but on the other hand, some people might say just for the sake of it that I was. [laughs] Do you follow me?

DC: Well absolutely. There's too much with Debra for us to believe any differently though. The handcuff key that we found in the parking lot.

TB: Yeah…

DC: So, we know you're not telling us a story there, we've got people who identified you being at the school that night too.

TB: Ok yeah well let's get back to the one, the young lady we were talking about.

DC: Nancy Wilcox?

TB: Mm hum.

DC: So she was walking along the side of the road, and you approached her and took her against her will?

TB: Yeah that's a good description. Yeah, basically. It was a fairly dark, particularly dark, stretch of road. It was a main roadway I mean, how do you describe it, but without any bullet streetlights. An old style, single bulb streetlight, ever three or four poles. So, it was dark. And ah, there was a, what looked like to be a small orchard. Very small, residential orchard between these two houses. And she was ushered into there, and restrained, and then placed in the car, and taken to the apartment.

DC: The park?

TB: The apartment.

DC: Oh, the apartment. And at what point would she have been killed? In the orchard, or at your apartment?

TB: The next day. The next day.

DC: Are we talking about the same apartment though?

TB: Yes.

DC: Do you recall anything unusual about her, anything that sticks out in your mind, as far as your… any scars, marks, or um… Obviously, did you know her name at that time?

TB: No, no I didn't.

DC: Did she talk about, was she able to talk about anything prior to the assault? You say you didn't have much of a conversation with her before.

TB: No.

DC: And where was she taken after the apartment?

TB: That's what I'm trying to remember. That's what I'm looking at, I need to look over this map. It's unclear to me right now.

DC: Well if I can help you, province is the one that goes straight east out of Salt Lake, and that's the main route to Park City, do you remember that one?

TB: Yes.

DC: And then of course, you go south to uh, you go to Point of the Mountain and you've got those small towns, Lehi, American Fork, and then Orem and then Provo.

TB: Mm hum.

DC: And north of course you've got Bountiful, Layton, other towns in that area as you go up to Ogden. Do you think it was, which direction do you think it was?

TB: Uh… south. My state of mind was not good then. I think I was… ah, I know I was not very lucid; I was new to the area. I sort of I got lost going to where I was going and got lost coming back.

DC: Did you follow 89 again or did you—?

TB: No, I went south, but how far south. Which, I don't, you know… It's not as clear as it was…

DC: With Debra?

TB: Yeah, the odd thing is, I remember contours. I remember ups and downs. And some other stuff. Ah…

DC: Well there's a lot of ups and downs in that area.

TB: This is true. A lot of 'em.

DC: You went south but you don't think you followed 89 that time?

TB: I sort of remember staying on the main drag, whatever that was. Not diverting at Spanish Fork, but continuing on, the main line, down, which is labeled as 91 here.

DC: This is quite an old map, because there should be a freeway, Interstate 15, that goes—

TB: Well this was some time ago itself; I don't know when this was published.

DC: You know…it was a freeway though?

TB: Well yeah you know, in those times you're right, it was a mixture, this is 1967 copyright. But at that time, it was a, a, ah, blend of construction, of 2 lanes, 4 lanes, back and forth… but a lot of it was two lanes, then, and it appears on this map as well a lot of it was two lanes.

DC: It was two lanes when this map was published.

TB: Going south but… time was not… you pass all these towns. You know how these little towns are. What would it be, Scipio, and Fillmore, and Meadow, and Kanosh, and everyone has those blinking orange lights and all the stores are dark. It's late at night, and you're just making sure you're obeying the speed limit because you know there's always a cop in that town gonna try to make his quota with you. But anyway, moving south… to Beaver… going, uh, west.

DC: Yeah, Beaver's a three to four-hour drive.

TB: Yeah that's not out of the question. It could've been Cove Fork, which is also, down far enough and has a western component to it.

DC: That's where Brigham Young used to have his summer home.

TB: What Cove Fork? Cove Fort?

DC: A little trivia there for you.

TB: How about that huh? Well you're not– if you were married by Reverend Musmann you're not Mormon, are you?

DC: No, no, no but I've…

TB: You can't help but know all that.

DC: Been out there 23 years.

TB: More or less… you know, indoctrinated.

DC: Yeah, they're trying. Musmann's fighting them off though.

TB: They're always at your door though, I know that. (laughing) Knock knock knock. Freshly scrubbed faces.

Good people, I mean, no question. They're wonderful people. Absolutely the best. That's what makes the place so nice. Even if you're not of that persuasion.

DC: Exactly. So, you think they're down in Beaver or Cove Fort?

TB: Somewhere down in that area. Farther off the road than that.

DC: To the left, or right?

TB: To the east, some distance.

DC: And there again, you just think it's in that general, you couldn't…

TB: I don't know. Sorry. You're catching me when you are.

DC: I'm just getting quite anxious myself.

TB: I hear you; I hear you. We're all up against some deadlines here. And ah, my mind's not as nimble as it used to be right now. Seems to me, it was something that went up and over something like a pass, pretty steep climb.

DC: A dirt road, or a paved road?

TB: No, a paved road. Four lanes. Could've been 4. Or 24. Goes up into the mountains. Does 70 cut through?

DC: Yeah 70's at four lanes. I mean, it is now.

TB: What was it back in 1974?

DC: Well I'd assume, probably a little bit of both. Yeah, 70 comes over and meets 15 now, and then… in fact, that's where they're picking up all the cocaine traffickers, down on Interstate 70.

TB: Ha ha. Why, why there?

DC: I don't know. The highway patrol for Utah is getting more cocaine than any other state, including Miami, or Florida. On that interstate. But anyway, you think it was a four lane, going east, paved road.

TB: Yeah. Up into the mountains. Pass.

DC: Did you follow that paved road quite a ways before you…

TB: No.

DC: See that eventually, you come go back into Price and can go back that way, if you follow 70 far enough. Did you make the circle, or?

TB: No. I think I came back the same way that I went down. I mean this was, late at night, 11, 12, 1 o'clock. And new area, dark. Obviously. New area. So, anyway, more or less picking whatever was available, not looking for anything marked on a map as much as just looking for something that's, uh…. a road suitably far off the beaten path. With some better maps, and knowing more about this 70, and a better description, a better description, or something, of this 24, might, I'm sure, would… as I remember…

DC: You're speaking of this road here?

TB: Yeah, 24. And what you indicated was later 70. Was going to be 70.

DC: So, it could be one of those two possibilities, is what you're saying.

DC: How far would you have traveled these do you suppose, on those paved roads?

TB: Oh… well into them. Huh. Could've been something like that. I want to find this place. I know it's there. I mean,

I know you could… well let's get there and I can tell you. On whatever side it's a mile to two miles down a graded dirt road, on the right-hand side, about 50 feet in. All of these are estimates. I can't be sure every time.

DC: But before you hit that dirt road, how far would you say you traveled east?

TB: I don't know. I wasn't looking for miles so much as I was trying to look for roads that appeared out of the dark alongside of this highway that looked like they went somewhere. And, uh… I remember one time, traveling, the reason I think it's 25, I remember one time traveling– but well again it might be wrong, it could be this 4 thing, if 70 went through–traveling this road and going to Green River, that is the Colorado Green River, and now I remember seeing this road, what looked like the road was going off to the right.

DC: You mean you traveled again, at a later time, and you recall that place?

TB: Right.

DC: And you were on your way to Green River?

TB: Right.

DC: Was that on your way up to Colorado you mean?

TB: Right.

DC: Miss Nancy, did you keep her approximately 24 hours at your place?

TB: Approximately. Yeah.

DC: Do you care to talk about cause of death there, how you caused her death?

TB: Well… it makes sense and it doesn't.

DC: Was a weapon used?

TB: No. No … someday it might, might be important but I think that for the family it's important that we find the body. That she died is unfortunate and real but uh, if we could find the body …

DC: Is there anything else then about where the body could be that you could tell me right now?

TB: Well… what did I tell you? I told you about the spot more or less.

DC: Yeah you weren't sure about 70 or … again, what was this highway number? But you thought you went over that road again on your way to Green River.

TB: We need better maps. That would help. We need just a clearer picture of what it looks like. I don't remember this Canyon Reef National Park but I don't imagine it looks any different from the rest of it except its name. I'm gonna take a break. Excuse me.

DC: Sure …

TB: Ah, this is uh, well, first of all, I know that you're not a reporter and that your job is to be a detective, and I would trust that to a certain extent you're not going to just run back to Salt Lake City and tell the press everything that I said … that you're more interested in solving the case, and letting the families know without reawakening all the pain by putting details in the paper that would …

DC: Absolutely. That's the first and foremost reason I'm here, for those three girls who are missing and …

TB: And some more.

DC: From Utah?

TB: Yeah. But, uh … it's way too late, and I've taken way too long, to come this far, but it's where I am now, and before it gets any later …

DC: You want to get it all out.

TB: Well that too, I need to get it all out, not just for you, but for these people here and for many people who aren't here.

DC: And for yourself too.

TB: Well …

Staff: Is this what you want? Cold water?

TB: Right, thanks. But to the extent … and in the event that anybody, especially families, want to know … I'm sorry. That doesn't correct a thing, but … I'm sorry. Not for me. I'm sorry.

DC: Well, by you saying that goes a long ways Ted.

TB: I-I'm not looking for anything. (*Author's note: Bundy is crying here, and it does appear to be legitimate and not for himself, but for the victims and the families*)

DC: I know.

TB: I understand now a lot of stuff, about myself, that I didn't understand then, and it makes me realize what was going on. It doesn't make it any less serious, but it … the senselessness of it, it appalls me all over, I'm sure not as much as those who are so close to it. Just as appalling however is the fact that I was so insensitive to it. One of many things that kept me from talking for so many years, and it doesn't excuse it, but uh … it's too bad I wasn't in a position to talk about this years ago. I still think though, that some good can come of this, especially at least in the case of the Kent girl. I hope that a serious attempt is mounted to find something.

DC: Well we got search and rescue on alert right now to try to do that, you know.

TB: Alright. Who does this, your sheriff's office or something?

DC: Yes, Pete Hayward, you know, he said to say hello, and wanted to know if you got his Christmas cards.

TB: I may have, I think I remember receiving one from him at one time. Yeah …

DC: He was the captain, and now he's the sheriff.

TB: Yeah …. Well I'm burned out and I'm sorry that I can't give you more, ah, especially on the second one, Wilcox. Let's see. Cause I know that this is a good chance, maybe in some ways a better chance, at finding it … the remains of … the young girl. I would uh, what's the scale? Let me look at this scale.

Staff: I could leave this with you, or would you not like it?

TB: Some of it, part of it. Not all of it, thanks. Ok. Try what I'd have to call on this map, the Notom Road, off Highway 24.

DC: You mean we're following this road and we take the Notom Road? Is that it there?

TB: To the right.

DC: Is this it here?

TB: No, no. Right there. See how it comes out … goes back …

DC: Right here?

TB: If I could see the actual entrance way, from several of these roads, what happens is on this particular road, you sort of, you make a right hand turn off … 24, go south for 100 feet or so, and then turn around, first to the right, and then a larger bend around to the left, which is a swooping kind of bend … it seems to be the way this Notom Road looks although it could be one of these others. But it's far enough in, I'd say it's far along Highway 24 to make some sense.

DC: But your recollection was, that you went over that road again on the way to Colorado, though, is that right?

TB: Yeah. One time, during the daytime.

DC: How far off of 24 then?

TB: I would say, within two miles, between a mile and two miles. On the right-hand side, up an embankment about 50 feet. Well, that's … your, your scale here says, uh …

DC: Well, I'm just putting a general vicinity type thing, on the right side …

TB: Well actually if you want to pinpoint it … I don't know about Notom, I never ran across Notom. I bet you there's probably, a uh, mailbox–

DC: That's a new one on me too there.

TB: You might want to look something on that X, more like a mile or two miles, and I think on the scale, 5, that's about 5 miles.

DC: Ok. Well, the clothing, did you discard kind of the same way … as Debbi Kent then?

TB: Yeah … yes, I did.

DC: Well, you cut the clothing up on the way back to Salt Lake?

Female voice: turn it off

TB: I ah, I'm not good for much more, for anybody. Not good right now.

Male Voice: As I said, I'm not trying to complicate you at all.

TB: Oh, I know you're not.

Male Voice: Washington and Colorado are basically saying "are we going to get our turn?" And if everything is basically going to be put this close together then we're gonna have five minutes than nothing. And of course, you're working as hard as you can, and he's working as hard as he can …

DC: Sure. Well ok we've done our best on those two, haven't we, Ted? Or can we do any more at this point in time?

TB: No … I mean well, I wish we could do better and we could do better I think if we had …

DC: Better maps?

TB: Better maps, that's important for the purposes certainly that I'm trying to accomplish.

DC: Can we go back to Nancy Baird, you indicated that …

TB: Nancy Baird … who's that?

DC: She's the girl from, uh, between Bountiful and Ogden.

TB: I'm not even sure … I don't even know why I was assumed …You said Nancy Wilcox I'm not sure I even know who you're talking about. Wait a minute, I'm not trying to cop out on you here, I mean, I'm getting a little confused. All these … uh …

DC: Well Nancy Baird, uh …

TB: Well I didn't even … did I describe—how did I describe Nancy Wilcox?

DC: Well you couldn't describe her clothing …

TB: Right. Ok. I believe it was casual, like blue jeans.

? Do you have a recollection of her physical appearance at all?

TB: Yeah, that's what I'm thinking … I want to make sure that I'm not getting names, just going for the name … uh, instead of also name the physical whatever … you see what I'm saying? Cause I didn't know the girl's name and I guess, I'm just reacting to publicity, somewhere along the line I heard the name Nancy Wilcox. Hell, I … I think … I hope what I said matches up. … unless the state of it is not good. Uh. I think I matched up the right name to the right incident because … only because I read about it sometime later in the paper and this was a long time later. Cause nothing came out in the paper about it for some time as I recall in this particular case which I later would associate with Wilcox.

DC: There wasn't that much publicity about it at the time.

Prison Staff: Mr. Couch, how much longer do you think you're going to be?

TB: Well we've just about had it with what we can do.

DC: Five minutes. Just five or ten minutes.

TB: Uh … There's more … I know there's much more to these cases and more to the other ones. Let me try to finish this Wilcox thing. Maybe it'll link it up a little bit better, because we want to make sure … that's … there is, that particular girl I mentioned that is here somewhere. The name, you'll find the name I'm sure if you find the remains. You should. I think it's Wilcox because that's just the name that attached to it some point later in time. That's all I can do right now.

DC: Ok, tell me about Melissa Smith, just a short synopsis. She was last seen right here in the Fashion Place Mall where you picked up Carol DaRonch, that's the last place she was seen.

(*Author's note: Bundy refuses to answer, lets out a sigh*).

DC: But you are responsible for Melissa Smith?

TB: (*long pause*) Just a minute.

DC: Sure.

TB: (*Very long pause; Bundy may be asleep*) Yeah … what's the question?

DC: Melissa Smith.

TB: Melissa Smith …

DC: Or Laura Aime, we can talk about either one, or both? With the time now that we have here.

TB: I just … listen. I know what you're doing. I know what you want. I know it. I understand why you're doing what you're doing.

DC: What, is the recollection getting to you or are you just burned out and …?

TB: I'm just having a hard time placing … the names are starting to get all mixed up.

DC: How about pictures, would they help you?

TB: Pictures never look anything like they really do. You can try … I mean, pictures I've seen in the newspapers but then again, they don't look like anybody I ever had anything to do with. What do you have?

DC: Well that was Debra Kent. Nancy Baird. This is Nancy Wilcox. Melissa Smith. You know, she was the chief of police's daughter. And then Laura Aime. Laura Aime and Melissa were the ones that we did find. Do you remember where you left them?

TB: Who? Oh.

DC: Laura and Melissa.

TB: We'll (*Very long pause*) have to do this some other time.

DC: Just think about Melissa and Laura if you have time … I'm not going to take this too far but can you give a general location of where you left them? What he's obviously trying to do is, you know, confirm the rest of it. If you can't, you can't, but I mean …

DC: How many in Utah are we talking about?

TB: I'm trying to count … we talked about, did we talk about that?

DC: No, uh-uh. I mean, I mentioned a figure and you said it was more than that.

TB: Yeah, that's right, it felt like it was more.

DC: Five. Yeah, well, I mentioned the fact that there was three missing, and he said there was more than that.

TB: Oh, yeah.

DC: How many more?

TB: Two.

DC: Anything about those two you can tell me?

TB: It was a teenage girl. I don't remember her name; I don't know who it was. It could have been one of these girls, I don't know which one she was. No, I don't think it was. I don't know the name. Damn.

DC: Would you like to talk to me again, do we have any more time between now and …

TB: Well, we, yeah, we need to talk again. If we have time. You need to get some better maps, if you can. And I need some sleep, my mind is just …

DC: Would you have Diana contact me again when we can arrange that?

TB: Yeah. She knows where you're staying?

DC: Yes.

TB: Ok. Yep. We'll work something out.

DC: Ok I appreciate the time tonight, Ted.

TB: Yeah, uh, I'm not bullshitting you. My mind … after a few of these my mind just seizes up. I mean I really, it's like I just can't say anymore, in some way. But we will get to them. I hope. All of them.

DC: Ok, anything you me want to tell Padre Musmann or anybody back in Utah?

TB: Yeah well … Lubeck. You ever see him?

DC: Yeah, he's a good man.

TB: Yeah, well say hello. Father Musmann. Does he remember … does he remember me?

DC: Oh yeah. Yeah.

TB: Played himself in that movie once … what was that?

DC: Oh, Gary Gilmore's, uh … He was quite taken in by your intelligence, though, and humor.

TB: Yeah, well, say hello. Please.

DC: Will do.

CHAPTER EIGHT

What follows is from my friend, Erin Banks. Although Erin lives in Hamburg, Germany, she has a great interest in Ted Bundy and other names in true crime. Very knowledgeable, she writes a blog aptly titled, CrimePiper. Because she lives in Europe, I asked if she'd like to contribute a piece for this book on how the rest of the world views true crime in general and Ted Bundy in particular, and thankfully she agreed.

Ted Bundy, heading to a court hearing, Utah 1976

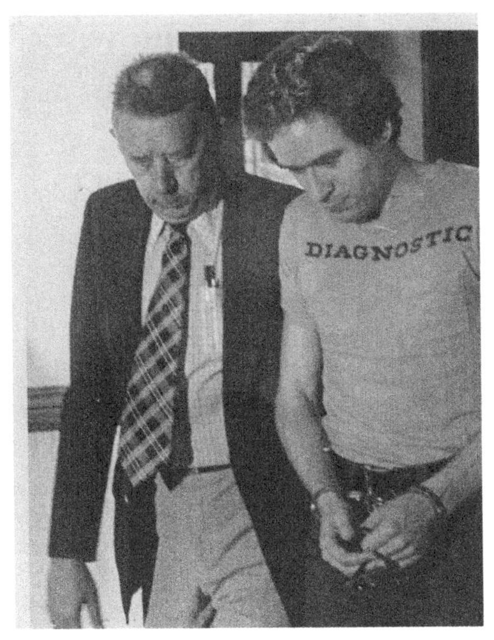

Bundy, on his way to court, 1976

HOW THE WORLD REACTS TO TED BUNDY

By
Erin Banks

There is no country which created a "serial killer culture" in equal measures as the USA did over the past four decades. It evolved in large part due to the creation of the FBI's Behavioral Science Unit entering the public consciousness. Cynics speculate that serial killers are an integral part of US popular culture because the American mindset is profoundly flawed; gun culture, the country's history of war and existence of the death penalty are to blame, they say.

In order to ascertain whether that claim holds up to scrutiny, I have taken several weeks to delve into Europe's, as well as the USA's, True Crime communities online, and so my overview is a general one and reflects my personal experiences and impressions.

A mere twenty years ago, True Crime was not only a niche interest in almost all of Europe, but one that fans of the genre spoke about in hushed tones, as it often roused suspicions whether those immersed in such a grim subject matter might be mentally ill, or even potential murderers themselves. With the advent of international streaming services, True Crime magazines being published globally, podcasts becoming widely popular and the market being saturated with books on individual cases, most of Europe was ultimately swept up by the hype. The genre was established as a mostly acknowledged and socially acceptable special interest that is nowadays more openly discussed among friends, family members, and even colleagues.

Within a comparatively short period of time, we had developed an equal fascination for morbid crimes, despite our overall lack of gun culture and the death penalty. It would appear that we must look elsewhere for an explanation for the phenomenon then. Perhaps it is reasonable to first consider human nature in general when examining possible motivations for the interest in True Crime.

When we sit in front of our computer conversing with others about Ted Bundy, for instance, illuminated only by the glow of its screen, it is oddly reminiscent of our ancestors sitting around a campfire to share horror stories with each other. A modern-day equivalent one might say.

The glue holding a society together is not solely made up of shared traditions, values, language, and spirituality but also the common hatred and fear of all that which could potentially damage or even destroy it. For centuries we lacked the framework to comprehend violent crime or specifically (serial) murder. Because of their bizarre nature, our forebears sought to fictionalize them, much like other cautionary tales about human nature were fictionalized into fables and parables. Serial killers became vampires, ghouls, witches, and other creatures of the night in horror folklore.

Whether fictional or real, such stories grant us the opportunity to feel normal, part of the society we were born into. If we move within the limits of our society, we believe ourselves adequately prepared, safe from harm. And likewise, we calculate that naming the unspeakable, making an honest attempt at explaining them, would do the same. If we learn how to detect and avoid all that or those who could kill us, one may argue that it also serves an evolutionary purpose.

For both Americans and Europeans alike, the above appears to be among the main motivations in immersing themselves in the subject. But both also show an increased interest in American serial killers. One reason for this is that Europe is still in its early stages of True Crime obsession, it is still transitioning from horror fiction to horror non-fiction so to speak, and orients itself along literature and online forums still more heavily dominated by Americans. We must also take into account the vastly different privacy laws in many European countries.

For instance, when German serial killer Thomas Holst escaped the psychiatric ward in 1995, he was referred to as "Thomas H." in national newspapers. Although his full name, Thomas Holst, has been known for many years, newspapers and literature still largely refer to him as "Thomas H." or by his moniker, the "Heath Murderer." This is, for one, because Germany is concerned that family members of the perpetrator and victims could be made a target by the general public. US cases such as the Golden State Killer, or even Chris Watts, have demonstrated how eager some in the True Crime community are to harass, dox, and intimidate innocent bystanders. Likewise, Germany's prerogative is to prohibit the outbreak of mass hysteria when publicly addressing national serial killer cases, one reason they are underreported and reports are oftentimes lacking in detail.

An understandable sentiment, once we remind ourselves of the panic the formation of the Behavioral Science Unit prompted in the American population. Initially, pressure on US law enforcement increased, more funding for the war on the alleged epidemic of serial murder was demanded, citizens began speculating about that one asocial neighbor that surely had to have *something* sinister to hide?

Most noticeable to me was that while in America, True Crime is equally consumed by people of all ages, ethnicities, political and religious affiliations, and from different social circles, European countries which are socio-politically more conservative, or in which traditional religious values still influence everyday life, are more often hesitant about the subject matter. This holds especially true for many Eastern European countries, and, albeit to a slightly lesser extent also the South, as well as Ireland.

On the other hand, Eastern European True Crime consumers, mostly young men, are more frequently prone to treating serial killers like rock stars or misunderstood folk rebels, and they may be more interested in declaring their interest publicly by wearing serial killer fashion, such as t-shirts. The rejection by the general population may be more understandable in that light. It was suggested to me that the reason for inadvertently lionizing killers in that manner may lie within the fact that for Eastern crime enthusiasts, their respective country's (recent) struggles or wars are still more fresh in their minds; a serial killer, to them, denotes a complete lack of boundaries and inhibitions. He is regarded the antithesis to all things conservative and restrictive, such as their governments, and is the epitome of complete freedom, revered, almost, in a similar fashion as their own rogue folk rebels who stood up to their regimes of old are.

In Southern Europe, there are interestingly more hybristophiles (those with a romantic and sexual interest in an offender) to be found in comparison. The women I spoke with decried the patriarchal structure of their individual countries and consider romanticizing criminals an utterly feminist endeavor, some of their favorites unsurprisingly including Ted Bundy, Richard Ramirez, or Jeffrey Dahmer, despite the latter's homosexuality. While I accept that this is their stance, I personally find it ironic to reinterpret hybristophilia as a subcategory of feminism, as it seems akin to a lamb not opting for freedom but rather choosing its own butcher.

Due to their persisting religiosity, both Southern European men and women also appear more inclined to consider certain supernatural aspects of individual cases, such as questions revolving around demon possession or an unseen spiritual warfare occurring between ordinary citizens and serial killers. One woman told me about her Ted Bundy "shrine" in great detail, complete with printed photos of the man, as well as a rosary pinned next to them. When I inquired as to the purpose of the rosary, she admitted that despite her fondness of Bundy, she still did not wish for him to feel invited to haunt her.

In Scandinavia and Finland, the fervor was initially—and to a small extent still is at times—tied to the subculture of Black and Death Metal. In the early 1990's, several band members did not only idolize any type of violence as per their lyrics, but went as far as murdering fellow band members or individuals completely unaffiliated with either scene. Old Stave Churches were burned to the ground, and a photo of Mayhem singer Per Yngve Ohlin's photo post suicide adorned one of the band's EP covers. Studying or researching True Crime wasn't the prerequisite, rather shock value was. Over the years, Scandinavia has increasingly separated the two fields again, and while one may find that a myriad of Metal fans are attracted to True Crime to this day, one cannot claim that the opposite holds true.

In Northwestern Europe, the preference conventionally bears more academic connotations. Individuals will more regularly refer to themselves as researchers, tend to focus on the psychopathology, speculation on a killer's motivation, modus operandi, and victimology. They may settle on one or a few limited cases. Ted Bundy being among the top killers of choice.

When asked why Ted Bundy, a substantial amount of them declared that their interest was awakened by the Netflix series, "*Conversations With A Killer: The Ted Bundy Tapes*," or that he had been the top result for their cursory Google and Amazon search on serial killers. And when going through the results, it had seemed easier to glean complete insight into his case, as there are not only a myriad of webpages and groups, but also dozens of books dedicated to Bundy, several by contemporaries and wayfarers of the man.

The French, similarly to the French Canadians, usually opt for a more isolated approach. There are fewer French True Crime fans to be found in international or US groups, as they prefer to discuss (mostly American) cases in their native language. The community is still relatively small, tightly knit, and revolves mainly around a handful of authors such as Stéphane Bourgoin, the man who interviewed Edmund Kemper in 1991, and wrote several books on individual serial killers over the course of approximately twenty-five years.

England had shyly embraced the subject for several more years than the rest of Europe, usually being the first ones to be overtaken by the latest American fad. They, too, had Metal bands such as Judas Priest ("Ripper" about Jack The Ripper), Venom ("Countess Bathory" about Erzebet Bathory) or Celtic Frost ("Into The Crypts Of Rays" about Gilles de Rais) broach the subjects in their songs, but similarly to the US, the distribution between the three major groups of scholars, hybristophiles, and anger excitation readers was more homogeneous from the very beginning.

Which takes us to one last group of True Crime consumers not previously mentioned. They appear to be distributed equally among Europe as well as the US—anger excitation readers. These are individuals who voraciously read and watch anything available on the subject of True Crime, yet employ the genre to vent their own personal frustrations. Indeed, it is, in its own curious way, their personalized brand of misunderstood anger management therapy. They harshly condemn not only hybristophiles but also those seeking to explain an offender's mental or emotional state to better comprehend crime and learn how to stop future offenders in their tracks. To them, this is a waste of time, as they cannot (or don't want to) detect the nuances between individual cases. It is of no consequences, whether one murderer suffered from psychosis, thus cannot even be held accountable for their own actions legally, or whether another chose to murder as a result of a neurodiversity, such as antisocial personality disorder. And every person disagreeing or offering scientific evidence to the contrary is considered an adversary, yes, even as morally corrupt as the offender himself. Death wishes and doxing are the main components of their self-righteous game. Not seldomly do the latter engage in the rather transparent attempt at elevating themselves, in certain cases fueled by the wish to conceal their own self-perceived moral transgressions.

It is my hope that, eventually, thorough studies will be conducted regarding the distribution of these main three groups of True Crime enthusiasts, and we can determine whether there is a similarly distinct difference of how the topic is approached in Europe as opposed to the US, or in other countries. To that end, the most desirable solution, in my view, would be for all main groups to develop a better understanding for each other, and accept that different people favor True Crime for different reasons, based on personal history and experiences, talents and preferences. We have much to learn from each other, and must learn from each other, if we would like for True Crime to persevere in the future.

ACKNOWLEDGMENTS

With every book written, no matter the century, there will always be people to thank. It's a given. As such, I would like to thank the following people, starting with those with whom I had the pleasure of working with at the beginning, in 2006 – 2008, and whose efforts are included within this book. Between the time when I wrote my first book, *The Bundy Murders*, published in 2009, and now, the numbers of my Bundy contacts (I consider them all friends) have thinned a bit with the passing of a number of them. Their efforts have, without question, made my books better books, and for that I will always be thankful:

The late Detective Jerry Thompson, formerly of the Salt Lake County Sheriff's Office, a good man who was generous with his time, sat for two interviews, and who always returned my phone calls, which says a lot; the late Ronald M. Holmes, who allowed me to come to his office and gave of his time to answer all my questions about his dealings with Ted Bundy; Don Patchen, lead detective in the Chi Omega murders for the Tallahassee PD, who, along with his wife, welcomed me into their Tallahassee home in late June 2008; my late friend, Jim Massie, who I'm indebted to for introducing me to Jerry Thompson, for without that meeting, there would never have been *The Bundy Murders*, and the following five books wouldn't exist either.

Thanks also to those who contributed their testimonies for this book: Susan Milner; Cheri Ranes; Michele Komen Nelson; and Scott Brainerd. A big thank you goes to Erin Banks for her fine piece on True Crime and Ted Bundy's impact throughout Europe. Thanks also to Shirl Sipperley DiGugno, who has been there for me whenever I needed her for a research project.

And to all of you who have read and enjoyed my books on Ted Bundy over the years, thank you! Your good feedback after each book was published, encouraged me again and again whenever the possibilities for a new Bundy project came before me. Thanks again.

Kevin M. Sullivan
July 14, 2020

For More News About Kevin Sullivan,
Signup For Our Newsletter:

http://wbp.bz/newsletter

Word-of-mouth is critical to an author's long-term success. If you appreciated this book please leave a review on the Amazon sales page:

http://wbp.bz/enigmabundya

Other Ted Bundy Books From Kevin Sullivan and WildBlue Press

wbp.bz/teottbma

wbp.bz/bundysecetsa

wbp.bz/trailbundya

wbp.bz/tbmma

See even more at:
http://wbp.bz/tc

More True Crime You'll Love From WildBlue Press

BOGEYMAN: He Was Every Parent's Nightmare by Steve Jackson
"A master class in true crime reporting. He writes with both muscle and heart." (Gregg Olsen, New York Time bestselling author). A national true crime bestseller about the efforts of tenacious Texas lawmen to solve the cold case murders of three little girls and hold their killer accountable for his horrific crimes by New York Times bestselling author Steve Jackson. *"Absorbing and haunting!"*(Ron Franscell, national bestselling author and journalist)

wbp.bz/bogeyman

REPEAT OFFENDER by Bradley Nickell
"Best True Crime Book of 2015" (Suspense Magazine) A "Sin City" cop recounts his efforts to catch one of the most prolific criminals to ever walk the neon-lit streets of Las Vegas. *"If you like mayhem, madness, and suspense, Repeat Offender is the book to read."*(Aphrodite Jones, New York Times bestselling author)

DADDY'S LITTLE SECRET by Denise Wallace
"An engrossing true story." (John Ferak, bestselling author of Failure Of Justice, Body Of Proof, and Dixie's Last Stand) Daddy's Little Secret is the poignant true crime story about a daughter who, upon her father's murder, learns of his secret double-life. She had looked the other way about other hidden facets of his life - deadly secrets that could help his killer escape the death penalty, should she come forward.

wbp.bz/dls

BODY OF PROOF by John Ferak
"A superbly crafted tale of murder and mystery."– (Jim Hollock, author of award-winning BORN TO LOSE) When Jessica O'Grady, a tall, starry-eyed Omaha co-ed, disappeared in May 2006, leaving behind only a blood-stained mattress, her "Mr. Right," Christopher Edwards, became the suspect. Forensic evidence gathered by CSI stalwart Dave Kofoed, a man driven to solve high-profile murders, was used to convict Edwards. But was the evidence tainted? A true crime thriller written by bestselling author and award-winning journalist John Ferak.

wbp.bz/bop

Made in the USA
Monee, IL
21 July 2022